MW00451041

THE 1935 MATANUSKA COLONY PROJECT

THE REMARKABLE HISTORY OF A NEW DEAL EXPERIMENT IN ALASKA

~ Helen Hegener ~

NORTHERN LIGHT MEDIA

The 1935 Matanuska Colony Project

The Remarkable History of a New Deal Experiment in Alaska

by Helen Hegener

© 2014 by Helen Hegener, Northern Light Media. All rights reserved.
No part of this book may be reproduced or transmitted in any form or by any means, electronic or mechanical, including photocopying, recording, or by any information storage and retrieval system, in whole or in part, without written permission from the author and publisher, except for the inclusion of brief quotations for the purposes of reviewing this book.

First printing 2014 by Northern Light Media.
Printed in the United States of America.

ISBN-10 0-9843977-8-7
ISBN-13 978-0-9843977-8-5

Additional copies available
for $24.00 postpaid from:
Northern Light Media
Post Office Box 298023
Wasilla, Alaska 99629

http://northernlightmedia.wordpress.com

The 1935 Matanuska Colony Project

In Alaska, it's sunrise–what a wonderful day!
On the mountains and valleys the wild flowers bloom gay,
And the joy of the earth, like a grand symphony,
Spreads a song o'er Alaska, with a sweet harmony.

~from Beautiful Alaska, by Don L. Irwin

THE 1935 MATANUSKA COLONY PROJECT

~

The Remarkable History of A New Deal Experiment in Alaska

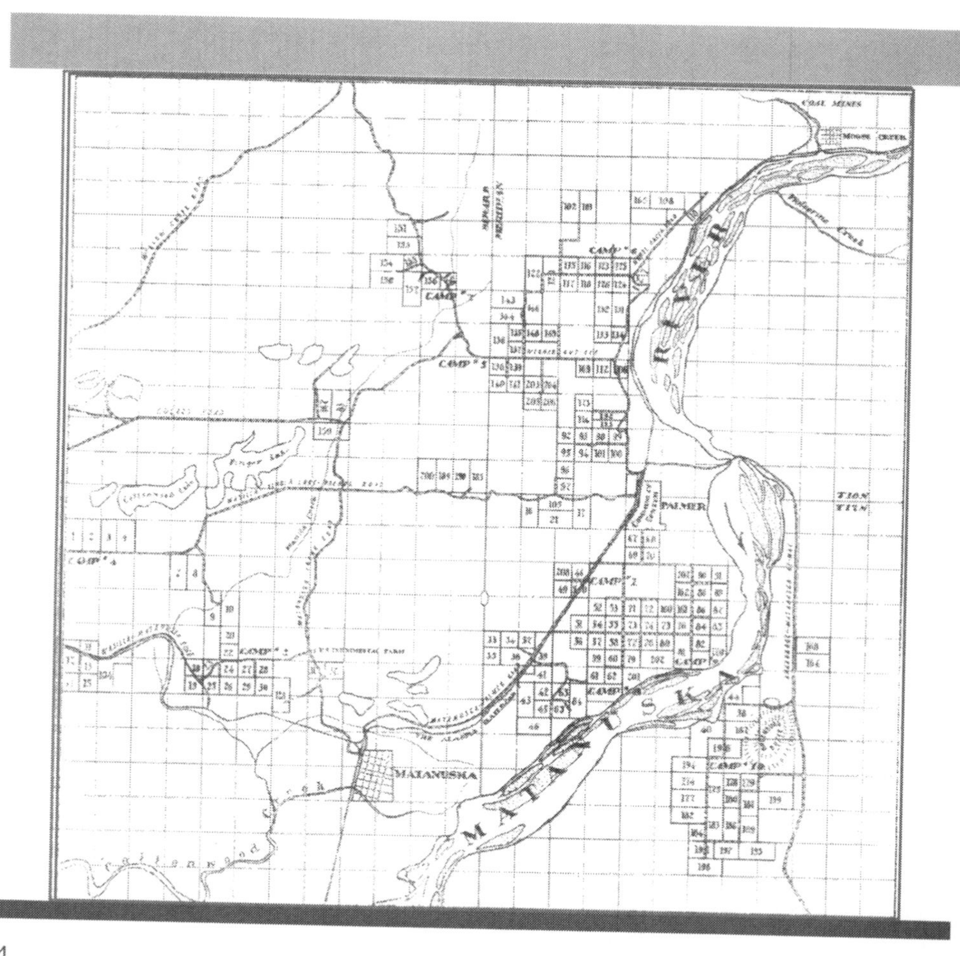

Mrs. E. Huseby in garden behind her tent home picking turnips, in the background can be seen the Huseby's cabin in construction and their cattle. ASL-P270-754 by Willis T. Geisman. ARRC Album, Mary Nan Gamble Collection, Alaska State Library.

The 1935 Matanuska Colony Project

Introduction

I have been keenly interested in the history of Alaska since the first time I travelled to the northland with my parents, in 1965. My father was a computer systems analyst with the U.S. Army, and we spent several years in Europe during my most impressionable years, from ages 6 to 12, when roaming the ancient castles and magnificent cathedrals of the Continent instilled in me a love and respect for history. Couple that with a girlhood passion for the tales of Jack London and Esther Birdsall Darling, and an interest in the history of Alaska was a natural consequence.

That natural bent to appreciate Alaska's history was nurtured by the many years I spent with two remarkable people: LeRoi Heaven and his sweet wife, Margaret. LeRoi was the son of a pioneer farmer, Foster L. Heaven, who had trapped along the northern edges of the Valley before turning his hand to farming. LeRoi spent many years as President of the Wasilla-Knik Historical Society, and his love for the history of the Valley was tangible and contagious. LeRoi was responsible for the rescue and rehabilitation of many of the Valley's early structures, including the McHenry cabin on his father's land, which was my home for years.

LeRoi's wife Margaret was the daughter of Hugh A. Johnson, a retired agricultural economist for the U. S. Department of Agriculture, a past Director of the Matanuska Experiment Station, and coauthor of the classic books, *The Land Resources of Alaska* (University of Alaska, 1963), and

Matanuska Valley Memoir: The Story of How One Alaskan Community Developed (University of Alaska/Alaska Agricultural Experiment Station, 1955). My treasured and well-worn copy of the latter book, in fact a side-stapled bulletin from the Matanuska Experiment Station, came to me from Hugh Johnson many years ago and was a primary resource for this book.

Perhaps the most important reason for my interest in this history is a simple one: This is my family's home; five generations of our family live here now. Not everyone in the family shares my absorption with what has gone before, of course, but history is a patient thing, and it will wait indefinitely for interest to arise. I hope that when my children, grandchildren, or perhaps even my great-grandchildren find an interest in the history of our Valley, they'll find my book an engaging one.

A note about this book: I have quoted and excerpted extensively from the few books which have been written about the Matanuska Colony Project, and from newspapers and other resources which relate to the history of this part of Alaska. In doing so I carefully studied the laws and guidelines of Fair Use, and I am confident that my usage falls within the acceptable parameters.

I prefer reading original sources to later interpretations whenever possible, and these books and other resources provide, in many cases, the only original written materials for this history. It is not my intention to usurp or disrespect the writing of those who recorded the Colony Project's history before me, but merely to make their important and valuable recordings and perspectives available to a new audience, and hopefully to encourage those with an interest in this history to seek out these original books and resources on the subject.

It is my hope that I have done justice to those writers and reporters who have gone before me, while providing information and inspiration to those who will come after.

Helen Hegener
Meadow Lakes, Alaska

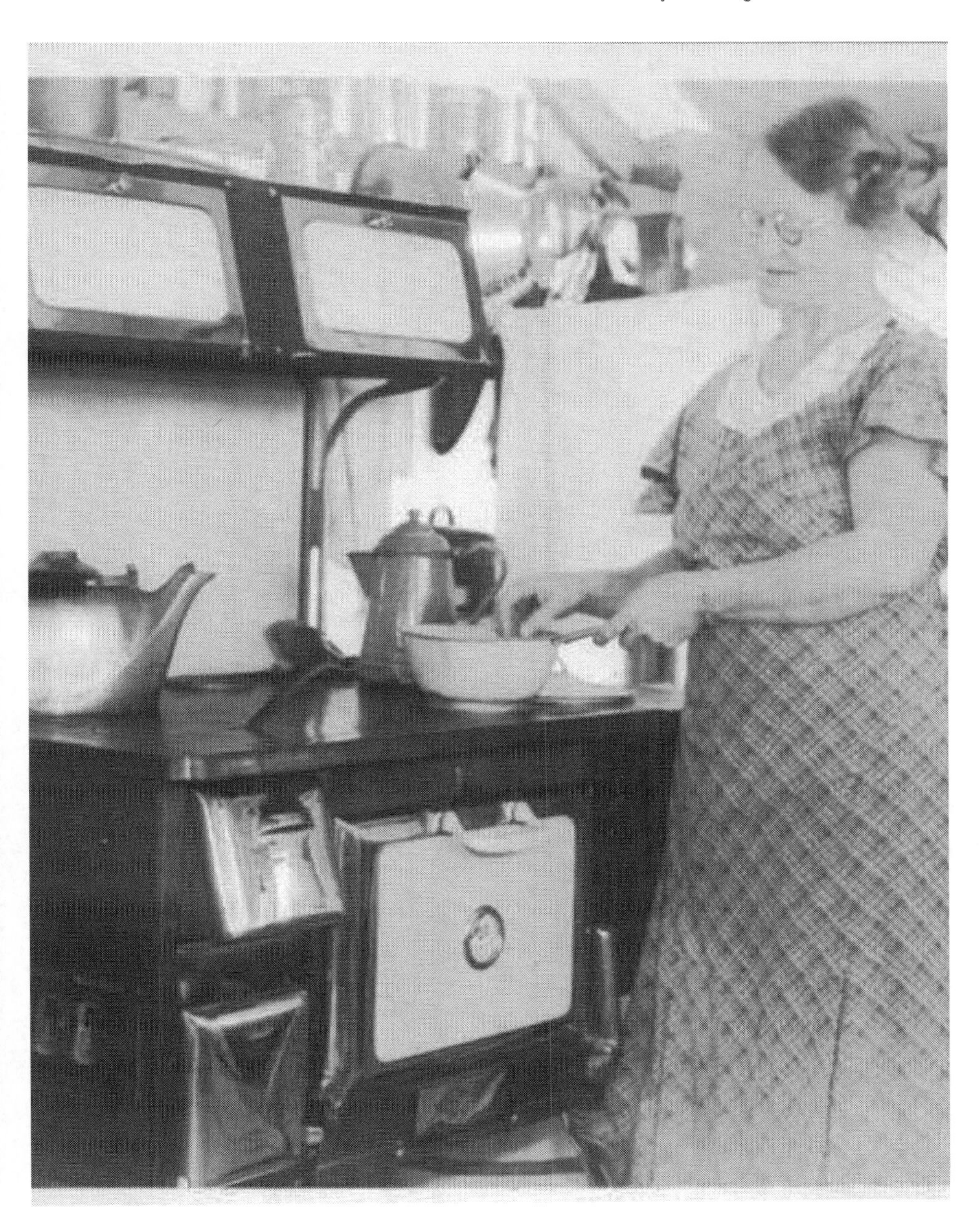

Mrs. Carl Erickson in her neat kitchen in her tent home in Camp 8. ASL-P270-646 by Willis T. Geisman. ARRC Album, Mary Nan Gamble Collection, Alaska State Library.

Pioneer Peak, six thousand foot sentinel that watches over Matanuska Valley. ASL-P270-667 by Willis T. Geisman. ARRC Album, Mary Nan Gamble Collection, Alaska State Library.

The 1935 Matanuska Colony Project

"No one person ever makes history." ~Hugh A. Johnson

Chapter One

A Context for Understanding

The history of Alaska is fraught with schemes for populating the state, from the first Russian attempts at colonization in the 1700's to the outlandish 1960's plan to build a domed city near Point Mackenzie, named John F. Kennedy City. That plan was researched by Julia O'Malley for her *Anchorage Daily News* column in February, 2010. She dug through the basement archives of the old *Anchorage Daily Times* and reported:

"On the last page of a dusty binder, I came across a clipping the size of a matchbox: 'Alaska Town is Re-Named JFK City.' It was date-stamped December, 26, 1963. The town had previously been called Bay City.

"In a proclamation on the name change, Mayor George Mor stated: 'John Fitzgerald Kennedy City is a new and frontier city which will rise as a great city ...' the article said.

"The population was 30."

There is no such place on the map today.

The 1935 Matanuska Colony Project was an audacious plan to move 200 hard-hit farm families from the drought-stricken upper midwest to new homes and farms in Alaska, then an only barely-settled frontier land. Farming in Alaska had been proven feasible by the U.S. government's agricultural experiment stations, the first of which was opened in 1898 in Sitka, which was at that time the capital of Alaska, by Dr. Charles Christian Georgeson.

The 1935 Matanuska Colony Project

Georgeson had been tasked with investigating Alaska's agricultural potential, and his work in opening several agricultural stations around the state marked the beginning of a substantial federal investment in Alaska.

Soon after the Sitka station, Georgeson oversaw the Kodiak Station opening, followed by another at Kenai in 1899. The following year, 1900, Georgeson toured other areas of Alaska and opened more experiment stations, including Rampart Station in the Yukon Valley and the Copper Center Station in the Copper River Basin in 1902. Each of these stations was tasked with exploring the agricultural potential of their region.

In 1902 the town of Fairbanks was established in the Tanana Valley, and in 1906 an experiment station was opened on a 1,400 acre site outside Fairbanks. The Tanana Valley became Alaska's first prominent agricultural area as farmers grew grain, hay, and vegetables, raised cattle and produced milk; the Tanana Valley was the center of agricultural production in Alaska until 1935, when the Matanuska Colony Project took shape.

Unfortunately, finding the funds to operate the experiment stations was a constant struggle and the Kenai and Copper River Stations both closed in 1908. The Rampart Station closed in 1925 after many years of successfully growing cereal crops.

In 1931 the Sitka and Kodiak stations closed and all of the remaining experiment station facilities were transferred from federal ownership to the Alaska Agricultural College and School of Mines at Fairbanks, renamed the University of Alaska.

Georgeson had opened a new experiment station in the Matanuska Valley in 1915 to help promote agriculture in the area at the same time the Alaska Engineering Commission was established to build a railroad from Seward to Fairbanks. The railroad was, in large part, intended to help agricultural development by making it easier to transport goods to market, and representatives of the Alaska Railroad worked to promote agriculture and attract new settlers to both the Tanana and Matanuska Valleys.

The Matanuska Valley had long been a favored land to the indigenous peoples, providing abundant rivers, creeks, and lakes for various types of fishing; forests, meadows, highlands and smaller Valleys for plentiful game and foraging of favorite foods and materials for clothing and shelters.

Framed on three sides by the towering Chugach and Talkeetna mountain ranges, the fourth side is open to the west and bounded along its southern edge by the tidal Knik Arm and glacial Knik River. The mighty Matanuska River enters the northeastern corner of the Valley and empties into Knik Arm in close proximity to the Knik River.

A trading station was established on the Matanuska River by early entrepreneur George Palmer, sometime between 1894 to 1898, to take advantage of the trails between the Cook Inlet region and the Copper River area. According to Wikipedia: "The indigenous Dena'ina-Athabascan name for the river is *Ch'atanhtnu*, based on the root -tanh 'trail extends out', meaning literally 'trail comes out river'."

In her small book titled *Old Times on Upper Cook's Inlet* (The Book Cache, Anchorage, 1967), Valley author Louise Potter describes the early trails through the Valley: "…the Indians must have marked walking trails through the Upper Inlet country well before 1898 and, after that time, prospectors brushed-out trail after trail, both winter and summer, leading from the coast to the coal and gold mines. Many of these trails were later widened for the use of dog teams and for saddle and pack horses and sleds. Eventually, some even became the government mail routes and, today, are busy roads."

Louise Potter continues, "A map of the Inlet area, copyrighted in 1899, shows eight such 'Trails Used by Natives…'" and she describes the one which probably led to the name "trail comes out river": "A summer trail from old Knik up the Matanuska River, passing 'Palmer's Upper House' (store) and King's House to Millich Creek and, via Hick's Creek, Trail Lake, and Nulchuck Tyon Village, to the Copper River (pretty much the route of the present Glenn Highway)."

In October of 1914, an Alaskan pioneer of Swedish descent named John August Springer filed for homestead rights to 320 acres of benchland located on the north bank of a sweeping bend in the Matanuska River, with a commanding view of Pioneer Peak and the Knik River Valley to the south and east, and the Chugach Range to the northeast. Springer built a log cabin and a few other buildings, and cleared and proved up on his land, receiving the patent in 1920.

Fifteen years later, in 1935, he sold a portion of his homestead to the United States government for $7.50 an acre, and his land became part of the Matanuska Colony Project.

According to Louise Potter in *Old Times on Upper Cook's Inlet*, John Springer was one of 132 people who were listed in the March 6, 1915 issue of the *Knik News* as having homesteads in the area. In describing early efforts by the pioneers, Potter explained the beginnings of agriculture in the Matanuska Valley:

"Before the coming of the railroad when pack horses were commonly used to haul freight from the waterfronts to the mines and when the railroad survey parties' horses were being wintered at Knik and Tyonook, it was necessary to do something about horse feed.

At Knik, for instance, fields were cleared for oats by 1904. The large area along the sea from Knik to Cottonwood and east became known as Hayflat as a result of the quantities of wild hay which were cut there. There were also several farms near the mouth of Ship Creek as early as 1911, St. Clair's and Whitney's among them."

In his 1968 book, *The Colorful Matanuska Valley*, Don L. Irwin, former superintendent of the Matanuska Experiment Station and General Manager of the Matanuska Colony Project, defined four distinct eras in the history of the Matanuska Valley. "First, the era of Russian and English voyages, discoveries, and exploration."

This began with Alaska's discovery in 1741 by Danish Captain Commander Vitus Bering, at the time serving the Russian Navy, and continued through 1844 with the first mapping of the Valley by Russian Captain Mate Molekoff. During the same era English Captains James Cook and George Vancouver were sailing the same waters; Captain Vancouver sailed to the head of Cook Inlet and explored the Matanuska Valley, but there is no record that he mapped his explorations.

The 1935 Matanuska Colony Project

The second era in Valley history, according to Irwin, was the beginning of development, which "might very properly be called the Prospector's and Trader's Era." The town of Knik grew and prospered with the many gold mines on Willow Creek, while coal fields north and east of the Valley were mapped by the U.S. Geological Survey, and the new Alaska Road Commission stayed busy opening the land to homesteaders.

This was the heyday of entrepreneurial traders like George Palmer, the first white resident of the Valley according to the 1880 census, whose trading station on the Matanuska River was established to take advantage of the trails between Cook Inlet and the Copper River area. Palmer would later open a mercantile store at Knik.

Orville G. Herning was another early businessman; in 1905 he built the Knik Trading Company, operating it in Knik until 1917, when he saw the wisdom of moving his business to the new railhead in Wasilla.

That railroad marked what Don Irwin identified as the third era, a time of change in the Valley as the town of Knik dissolved into history's archives and the new town of Wasilla received a post office and a U.S. Deputy Commissioner's office which was tasked with the recording of marriages and mining claims.

Palmer, which was then known as Warton because the postal system would not accept the name Palmer, was only a railroad siding on the branch line to the Jonesville coal mines at Sutton and Chickaloon. There was a freight warehouse and a post office, and a handful of nearby homesteaders, including the aforementioned homesteader John August Springer. Irwin described the situation in 1934:

"There was no highway from the Valley into Anchorage. The Glenn Highway had not yet been surveyed. Train service was the only means of travel out of the Valley. There were no regular church services in the Matanuska Valley from 1918 to 1935. The volume of produce raised by the farmers was too small to interest the Anchorage merchants. The U.S. Agricultural Experiment Station at Matanuska began operation in 1915. A steel bridge was constructed across the Matanuska River near Palmer in

1934. The nearest physician, hospital facility and U.S. Deputy Marshal were at Anchorage. The economy of the Valley seemed to be marking time."

Irwin's fourth era was, of course, that which followed the 1935 Matanuska Colony Project. With the influx of 203 families - and the attendant financial resources provided by the Federal Government - the changes came swiftly. Roads were improved, extended, and eventually paved; bridges spanned the rivers, and freight and passenger trains established schedules. Schools and libraries were built; retail stores, supply services and other businesses were developed; cooperative electric and telephone systems took shape, and a network of churches arose, with many different faiths represented.

There have since been other significant eras which helped to mold the Valley, such as the building of the trans-Alaska pipeline and the influx of new settlers and businesses which came with those boom times, but the historic importance of the Matanuska Colony remains evident.

Today the Alaska State Fair utilizes several original Colony buildings for administration and exhibit purposes, including a beautifully preserved Colony barn, one of over 60 remaining Colony barns in the Valley. These photogenic historic landmarks can be found in many different states of repair, from well-restored and still functional to collapsed and decaying slowly into the ground. Almost all were built from the same blueprint designed by David R. Williams, and their three-sided log first floors topped by a broad gambrel roofline with a bell-cast lower pitch make them easy to identify.

Seventeen structures have been identified within the National Register of Historic Sites' Matanuska Colony Historic District, including several Colony farms, a number of original Colony homes, the Matanuska Colony Community Center, the Palmer Train Depot, and others.

The Colony House museum in Palmer, originally the home of Colonists Oscar and Irene Beylund on tract number 94, north of Palmer, reflects an average Colonist family's home, restored to its 1936 -1945 appearance. Administered by the Palmer Historical Society, the living room is features furniture from the 1930's and 40's era, including some original to the home. The bright cheerful kitchen includes many unique items utilized by Colony housewives, and throughout the home can be found old books, games and photos which were donated by families of the original colonists.

Perhaps most significantly, the town of Palmer still reflects the planning of government architect David R. Williams, whose unique design for the aforementioned Matanuska Colony Community Center still functions as the town's core, with three sides of an open central area anchored by buildings which were originally the large three-story school (now the Matanuska-Susitna Borough offices), the teacher's dormitory (now the Colony Inn), and the trading center (now a restaurant).

The grassy park, now featuring historic signs telling of the town's Colony heritage, is a favorite gathering place. Nearby is the ship's bell from the U.S. Army Transport Ship *St. Mihiel*, which transported the first group of colonists from Minnesota to Alaska, and a set of brass plaques with the names of the Colonist families. The inscription on the first plaque reads:

"50th Anniversary. Matanuska Valley Colony Project. Honoring the 202 families from Michigan, Wisconsin, and Minnesota who braved the migratory transition from the depression-torn years of strife and struggle to the promised lands of the fertile Matanuska Valley, and in their endeavor, with faith, hope, and courage, created a new life filled with challenging goals, bringing to Alaska the permanency of residency, the maturity of agricultural development and the true reality that Alaska held the future for the generations to come. Their sacrifices and hardships, together with their gallant leadership has brought greatness to Alaska. May their generations never die. 1935-1985."

"This is a strange land." ~David Williams

Chapter Two

A History of the Land

In *Exploration of Alaska 1865-1900* (University of Alaska Press, 1992), Morgan B. Sherwood notes, "An early mention of the agricultural value of the Matanuska Valley appeared in Glenn's report."

The "Glenn's report" referred to was that of Captain Edwin Forbes Glenn, the U. S. Army officer in charge of explorations in south-central Alaska in 1898 and 1899. Captain Glenn's descriptions of his expedition are a fascinating look at the earliest official incursions into the Cook Inlet and Matanuska regions:

"We rounded Cape Elizabeth in the early morning of May 31, and consumed the remainder of the day and until nearly midnight in reaching Tyoonok, at which place we found scattered along the beach from 200 to 500 prospectors, about 100 Indians (men women and children) and the trading station of the Alaska Commercial Company. This place is generally considered to be the head of navigation in Cooks Inlet, but I subsequently ascertained that excellent anchorage, plenty of water, and a safe harbor, were obtainable at Fire Island, which is situated between the mouths of Turnagain Arm and Knik Inlet, a distance of about 18 miles farther up the inlet."

"On this date (June 1), having discharged Guide Howe, I secured as guide Mr. H. H. Hicks, who had been for three years prospecting up the

An old sourdough's cabin. ASL-P270-638 by Willis T. Geisman.
ARRC Album, Mary Nan Gamble Collection, Alaska State Library.

Matanuska River, with which country and the Indians located on or near the same he was very familiar, having traded with them during his entire residence in Alaska."

"The five animals sent me having had sufficient rest, and believing, from the best information obtainable, that an outlet into the interior could be found via the Matanuska River, I decided to send Lieut. J. C. Castner, U. S. A., with Mr. Hicks as guide and a sufficient number of enlisted men, up this stream for the purpose of cutting a trail as far as practicable before the mules needed and called for arrived."

"We reached Knik Inlet finally, cast anchor, and waited for the vessel to go aground before attempting to unload. We were deeply impressed with the appearance of everything in this inlet. The weather was much more mild than in the lower part of the inlet, and the season more advanced than at Tyoonok or at Ladds Station by at least three weeks. The trees were in almost full leaf, and the grass a sort of jointed grass resembling the famous blue grass of Kentucky was abundant and at least a foot high. The length of this arm is about 25 miles. Coming in at the head of it were the Matanuska and Knik rivers, the former from the east, the latter from the south. The valley there is quite flat and about 20 miles across. In fact, the valleys of both streams are in full view from just above the trading station.

"This inlet, when the tide goes out, seems to be an immense mud flat. I learned from reliable sources that about two years ago the navigable channel of this inlet passed directly in front of and close to the trading station. But it seems that at that time an immense body of water came down, apparently from the Knik River, destroying not only the trading establishment of the Alaska Commercial Company, located on the opposite bank of the inlet, but also a number of Indian houses. The Indians say that as this flood came down it presented a solid wall of water at least 100 feet high. This statement, however, should be very much discounted. At any rate, the effect, in addition to the destruction of the houses, was to leave deposited in front of the present trading company's establishment an immense amount of mud and sand that extends out from the shore for nearly if not quite half a mile, and prevented us from landing at the station. We were forced to cast anchor at the mouth of the small stream, 2 miles below, that is used by the Knik Indians during the fishing season."

The "immense body of water" referred to by Captain Glenn was well-documented as a significant event in the Valley's history. In *Shem Pete's Alaska: The Territory of the Upper Cook Inlet Dena'ina* (University of Alaska Press-Fairbanks, 1987), the flooding is mentioned:

"Just before 1900, three Indian villages along the Knik River were destroyed by a great flood, which was believed to be the result of the breakout of Lake George. No previous flood damage along the Knik River had been recorded, although the lake emptied once every 15 to 20 years according to Indians living in the area."

Lake George, a glacial lake formed near the face of the Knik glacier, received national recognition by the National Natural Landmark Program because of a unique natural phenomenon called a "jökulhlaup", an Icelandic term for glacial lake outburst flood. The intermittent breakup of the lake's ice dam would send a violent wall of water, ice and debris down the river valley causing massive flooding and sometimes devastation to local settlers' properties. The Lake George jökulhlaup has not occurred since 1967, due in part to glacial recession, but also for reasons associated with the massive Good Friday Earthquake of 1964.

W. C. Mendenhall, a member of Captain Glenn's expedition, made the first rough geological survey of the Matanuska Valley. According to the 1912 U.S. Geological Survey bulletin, *Geology and Coal Fields of the Lower Matanuska Valley, Alaska*, by George Curtis Martin and Frank James Katz:

"The Matanuska Valley was traversed in 1898 by W. C. Mendenhall, who was attached as geologist to 'military expedition No. 3,' in charge of Capt. Edwin F. Glenn, Twenty-fifth Infantry, United States Army. Mendenhall's explorations covered areas on the west shore of Prince William Sound and a route extending from Resurrection Bay to the head of Turnagain Arm, thence by way of Glacier and Yukla Creeks to Knik

Arm, up the Matanuska Valley to its head, and thence northward to the Tanana. Mendenhall's account of his explorations includes a description of the general geologic and geographic features accompanied by a topographic map on the scale of 1 to 625,000."

Under the heading General Description of the District, the Matanuska River is described:

"Matanuska River is tributary to Knik Arm, at the head of Cook Inlet. It rises on the western edge of the Copper River basin and flows between the Talkeetna Mountains on the north and the Chugach Mountains on the south. The Matanuska is about 80 miles in length and has a drainage basin of about 1,000 square miles. Its fall in the part of its course included in the area here described in detail is about 20 feet to the mile. This rapid fall gives it a swift current, because of which and of its being overloaded with sediment and consequently being in most places broken up into many shifting channels over an aggrading flood plain, it is not navigable. The fall is, however, so evenly distributed that there is no available water power. The principal tributaries of the Matanuska are Caribou Creek, Hicks Creek, Chickaloon River, and Kings River, of which the last two enter it within the area here described in detail. The other tributaries which it receives in this area are Coal, Carbon, Eska, and Moose creeks. It is a noteworthy fact that tributaries of the Matanuska all enter it from the north."

After a couple of paragraphs describing the relative heights and characteristics of the mountains and the Matanuska River, Mendenhall's report turns to vegetation in the Valley proper:

"Timber line in this area is at a general elevation of 2,000 to 2,500 feet, above which there is the customary growth of small bushes, moss, and grass. The trees include spruce, birch, and several kinds of cottonwood. The growth is in general not dense. Most of the spruce trees are under 12 inches in diameter, the largest one which the writers noted having a circumference of 5 feet. The timber is probably sufficient for any local demands that can now be foreseen, provided that forest fires which the dry climate favors are kept under control. There is no timber suitable for export. The more open birch forests, as well as the areas which have lately been burned, are covered with a dense growth of grass. These natural meadows are large enough to furnish feed for whatever stock is likely to be locally needed."

Mendenhall's report then describes accessibility of the Valley:

"The Matanuska Valley is at present reached from Knik, which is the head of navigation on Cook Inlet, and to which vessels of shallow draft can go at high tide. Near the lower end of Knik Arm there is a good anchorage, which ocean going vessels can reach at any stage of the tide except during the winter, when the whole upper part of Cook Inlet is frozen.

"There is a good horse trail from Knik to the upper end of Matanuska Valley, and the character of the ground and of the vegetation is such that this trail could be made into a wagon road at comparatively slight expense. It takes horses from one to two days to reach Moose Creek, depending on the load, and from a day to a day and a half to go from Moose Creek to Chickaloon River.

"At present freight can not be taken in while Cook Inlet is frozen, which is usually from October 15 to May 15, and passengers can reach the region during the winter only by going in from Seward with sleds.

"The Alaska Northern Railroad, which is now completed from Seward to Kern Creek, on the north shore of Turnagain Arm, a distance of 72 miles, is intended to reach Matanuska Valley, to which surveys have been made; some construction work has been done between Kern Creek and Knik Arm. According to the present surveys it will be about 150 miles from Seward to Chickaloon River. When this road is completed the Matanuska Valley will be easily accessible at any time of the year."

Joe Kircher's farmstead circa 1930 two larger buildings are out of photo. ASL-P270-705 by Willis T. Geisman. ARRC Album, Mary Nan Gamble Collection, Alaska State Library.

"I am, however, still a cheechako–Alaskan term for beginner–because, for one thing, I have not 'seen the snow come all the way down the mountains and then go back up again.'" -Kirk H. Stone

Chapter Three

Matanuska Valley, Pre-Colony

The earliest enterprises in the Matanuska Valley were focused in the Talkeetna Mountains, in the form of gold mining in the Willow Creek Mining District, and the development of coal fields near Chickaloon and Sutton. In *Old Times on Upper Cook's Inlet*, Louise Potter described the progress of early gold mining:

"The Willow Creek District off the Big Susitna River, which later proved to be the center for so many of the Inlet's successful mines, had but four men working claims during the early spring of 1898: 'Doc' Herndon, Billy Morris, E. Brainerd, and Capt. Albert Andrews. However, by the middle of May, 1898, 300 prospectors were reported to be camping on the beach at Tyoonok. These, plus others who came later that season and the next, not only swelled the numbers working in the Willow Creek District but were scattered throughout the creeks of the whole Upper Inlet region..."

Gold prospecting in the Matanuska Valley reached its peak in 1919, although an increase in the value of gold a dozen years later spiked activity between 1933 and the beginning of World War II.

Local Athabascans had told early prospectors and fur trappers about the coal fields in the hills above the Matanuska River, and in 1898 Captain

Glenn's Army exploration party found a vein of good quality coal that measured four feet across near the Chickaloon River. Fifteen years later, in 1913, interest in the coal fields was driven by the U.S. Navy seeking a source of coal for refueling the Pacific Fleet without needing to return to the United States.

The USS Maryland conducted tests on 1,100 tons of bituminous coal from Chickaloon and found it had good burning properties and would be acceptable fuel for ships, and in the years following a thriving community developed, the town of Chickaloon, which had homes, a school, stores, a power plant, dormitories, and a mess hall.

In 1919, more than 4,000 tons of coal were mined. Two years later, the Navy began building a million-dollar coal-washing station at nearby Sutton. All of the coal that Chickaloon mines produced over the next few years was for Navy use, and not even the government railroad could burn the coal from Chickaloon.

Around the same time the Navy was planning to enlarge the mines, California oil was found to be more economical than coal, and ship engines were converted to burn oil instead of coal. Not long after, the Navy ordered the mine shut down.

Providing food for the early gold and coal mine workers spurred clearing and planting of the first farmsteads in the Valley. The rich soil and moderate climate were conducive to many crops, as shown in photos of early farms. In *Matanuska Valley Memoir*, Bulletin #18 from the Alaska Experiment Station, July, 1955, authors Hugh A. Johnson and Keith L. Stanton describe early farming development: "Agriculture in the Valley came into its own in 1915. Most of the 150 settlers filing for homesteads came intending to farm. Some cleared enough land to put in a crop the next year. Settlement was concentrated in the vicinity of Knik, across the Hay Flats and up the Matanuska River with a few homesteads spotted along the trails leading to Fishhook Creek. The greatest influx of settlers occurred in 1916 and 1917. By the end of that period nearly all the available land had been homesteaded--a fact not commonly known."

The 1935 Matanuska Colony Project

The chief outfitting point for the Matanuska and Susitna Valley gold mines was Knik, the largest town and the main port on the Inlet, reported to have a population of 250 people in 1914. In *Matanuska Valley Memoir* Johnson and Stanton wrote about the town's growth:

"The two years 1914 and 1915 were Knik's golden years. The town was small but, because of its importance as a transportation center, it boasted four general merchandise stores, two hotels, two transfer companies, two combination bakery-restaurants, one law office, one billiard hall, one bar, one candy shop, one barber shop, one contracting firm, one newspaper, three qualified doctors and two dentists. A U.S. Comissioner also resided in Knik, but there was no deputy marshall. The marshall for the third district resided in Valdez."

Johnson and Stanton added that while the Valley lacked law enforcement officers, it was "singularly free of crime. There is no record that a miners' meeting for law enforcement was ever held in the Matanuska Valley."

In *Old Times on Upper Cook's Inlet*, Louise Potter printed a list of 132 people who had homesteads near Knik in 1915, noting, "That such a list is possible at all is apt to come as a surprise to many who have been encouraged to believe that 1935, the date the 'Colonists' arrived in the Matanuska Valley, marks the beginning of the history of agriculture in the Upper Inlet Region..."

In fact, George Palmer had been experimenting with the seeds he received from the Sitka Agricultural Experiment Station since 1900, when he wrote the following letter to Prof. C.C. Georgeson detailing his efforts at Knik:

"Dear Sir:

"Your favor of July 17 just reached me. When you learn that the nearest postoffice (i.e. Sunrise) is about 80 miles from here, and that I have to go in a small sailing boat, in perhaps the most dangerous water on the coast for small boats, you may know that I take a trip only when necessary; so my mails are few and far between. I have received no seeds yet, and it is hardly likely that another mail will reach me this fall, as navigation will soon close for the winter.

"In regard to the seeds I planted last spring, will state that my knowledge of gardening is very limited, but have had very fair success so far. I have less than an acre in cultivation.

"Parsnips are the finest and largest I ever saw, and the first I have heard of raised in the vicinity.

"Turnips grow to an enormous size, and of fine flavor. (Captain Glenn took a sample of my turnips last year to Washington.) This year my seeds were bad in some way, as most of them went to seed. I don't know the reason why.

"The Scotch Kale is a perfect success here. Two men who came here from where it is raised extensively say it was the finest they ever saw.

"Cabbage is small, but heading fast at present. They have heads about the size of a pineapple cheese, and are of a fine flavor.

"Rutabagas are large and fine; have just taken mine into the root house. I had some so big that three filled a 30-pound candy pail.

"Lettuce, peas, radishes, cauliflower, and potatoes are a success.

"I made a failure of cucumbers, tomatoes, spinach, and parsley, and a partial failure of onions, but I think they could be grown from seed.

"The natives above raised some potatoes, turnips, kale, cabbage, cauliflower, parsnips and radishes. They are very anxious to learn. I am a very poor teacher, as I must learn myself before I can teach others. Instructions about planting should go with all the seeds you send out. Some of the failures were due to my inexperience.

"Yours, truly, G.W. Palmer."

By 1906, farmers Henry McKinnon and Hiram Mitchell were both producing large gardens near Knik and selling their surplus produce to the miners and villagers. Others settled in the area near present-day Palmer, including pioneer farmers John A. Springer, Adam Werner, W.J. Bogard, M.D. Snodgrass, John Bugge, Jake Metz, Swan Youngquist, Ira Miller, A.J. Swanson, Max Sherrod, and many more. By 1915, there were enough farms in the Valley to support the formation of the Matanuska Farmer's Association, as described in the April 10, 1915 issue of the Valley's first newspaper, the *Knik News*:

"As indicating the enthusiasm with which the homesteaders are entering into the matter, fifty-three settlers attended the second meeting of the Matanuska Farmer's Association, held Sunday last at the home of George Nylen. The meeting proved a fine success as it brought the homesteaders together for a discussion of things of mutual aid and benefit..."

It was the Colonists' good fortune to land in a dramatically beautiful Valley which already had a rich and vibrant history, and they contributed hard work and dreams of a better future to help build it into a dynamic and vibrant place. But Alaska had been advertised and promoted to farmers for many years before the Colonists headed north.

In an article for the *Pacific Northwest Quarterly*, October, 1978, which was later reprinted in the anthology *Interpreting Alaska's History*, James R. Shortridge wrote about the many government and private efforts to promote Alaska as an agricultural Promised Land: "...almost every promoter lauded the long summer days and their amazing effect on vegetable quality and size. One enthusiast called the tropical sun 'too intense' for best plant growth whereas 'the slanted light of the higher latitudes is always soft and delicate, stimulating growth and not retarding it.' According to some, these magical conditions impart to Alaskan produce 'such superior flavor that when a person has once eaten the vegetables grown in Alaska, other vegetables are insipid and tasteless.'"

Johnson and Stanton's *Matanuska Valley Memoir* goes into detail about the early agricultural developments in the Valley, and explains how the history unfolded: "When the 1917 season rolled around approximately 400 settlers prepared to plant a larger crop than ever before. The Matanuska Farmer's Association's building was ready for use in Matanuska Junction; construction on the railroad was proceeding at a rapid rate. The Alaska Road Commission had completed a new road from the Little Susitna Valley through Wasilla to Knik. Other plans called for constructing a network of roads to replace trails then in use.

"Prosperity seemed certain as the farmers took to the fields those first days of May 1917. But with the entry of the U.S. into World War I, Alaska was left in a state of almost complete stagnation. The war profoundly affected the Matanuska Valley.

"Alaska's manpower answered the call to duty with characteristic enthusiasm. Men left undeveloped farms, unfinished construction, partially developed mines and industries. Railroad construction suffered immediately from lack of funds, scarcity of materials and lack of manpower. When the harvest was completed in September of 1917, the market had shrunk and a ruinous surplus of potatoes and vegetables resulted. The potato crop for 1917 was estimated at 1,300 tons. There still remained 600 tons of unmarketed potatoes in the spring of 1918. These were lost because there was no livestock to eat them.

"Because of this unsold surplus, many farmers failed. Swan Youngquist was reported to be the only farmer who made money in 1917. He sold directly to Anchorage residents. The Farmer's Association was dissolved in 1918 and its debts were assumed by several men in the Valley, among them F.F. Winchester and Al Waters. Farming was too undeveloped and lacked reserve capital to survive these adversities. By 1920 less than 200 settlers remained in the Valley. Not until the Colonists arrived in 1935 did agriculture again move ahead."

Despite this dismal picture, there were encouraging developments in the Valley's agricultural scene, starting with the building of the Matanuska Experiment Station in 1918. Once again Johnson and Stanton give a very detailed report in *Matanuska Valley Memoir*:

"M.D. Snodgrass, on the Alaska Engineering Commission's recommendation, chose section 15, township 17 north, range 1 east of the Seward Meridian, which originally consisted of 240 acres as the location for the Matanuska Experimental Farm. Section 14 adjoining the 240 acres was later set aside for the station, making a total of 880 acres to be developed for experimental purposes. For the fiscal year ending June 30, 1918, $10,000 was appropriated for the station and work was begun under the direction of F.E. Rader on April 1, 1917.

"The first three years were spent in clearing land and erecting buildings. As soon as land was cleared, Rader began testing varieties of potatoes and grains. He also maintained a garden and nursery. Some machinery was placed on the farm."

The somewhat dry report goes on and on, detailing the Experimental Farm's testing of varieties of crops and grains, the participation of the farmers in the testing, problems confronting the homesteaders, individual stories of several successful farmers, and how the high freight costs and finding suitable markets was handled.

In 1920 the Experimental Farm began working with cattle, starting with five milking Shorthorns, then adding six Galloways from Kodiak and Holsteins which were cross-bred with the Galloways to develop a strain of dual-purpose cattle who could withstand rigorous Alaskan winters while being suitable for both beef and dairy production.

Also introduced by the Experimental Farm in 1920 was a flock of 16 Cotswold sheep: "This introduction interested several farmers in the sheep enterprise and they bought most of their foundation stock from the Station flock. By 1930 three farmers owned 221 sheep. W. Bogard, whose homestead was on the north shore of Finger Lake, owned the largest flock."

By the late 1920's several farmers had developed small dairy herds, and a cooperative arrangement between the Alaska Agricultural Stations and the Alaska Railroad resulted in the construction of a creamery at Curry, which meant a new market for the milk produced in the Matanuska Valley. While the remote community at mile 248 of the Alaska Railroad may have seemed like an odd choice for the creamery, its grand hotel was a popular and respected stop, and Curry included cottages, a train depot, a bakery, the railroad shops and bunkhouses, and a large commercial laundry; all of the laundry for the Alaska Railroad and the hospitals at Nenana and Anchorage went through the huge facility at Curry.

The 1935 Matanuska Colony Project

The opulent Curry Hotel was described in Ken Marsh's 2003 book, *Lavish Silence: A pictorial chronicle of vanished Curry, Alaska* (Trapper Creek Museum Sluice Box Productions, Trapper Creek, Alaska 2003): "The Curry Hotel, first opened in 1923, boasted amenities in a wilderness setting seldom seen even in large stateside establishments during this time. Tennis courts, a golf course, a swimming pool, a footbridge spanning the rolling width of the Susitna River and a winter ski lift, all helped make Curry world famous. Nothing was lacking for human enjoyment and comfort."

Marsh described the creamery as well: "Another Curry-based enterprise was operated for the benefit of farmers to encourage dairy farming along the Alaska Railroad. A creamery that turned out 1,434 pounds of butter in July and August of 1932, also made ice cream, table cream, buttermilk, cottage cheese and sweet milk. The dairy products were used at the Curry Hotel, in the Alaska Railroad dining cars, and Base Hospital at Anchorage. Other merchants purchase surplus products. The churns of the creamery were later moved to the Experiment Station at Matanuska since most of the cream came from that area as time went by."

While the completion of the 500-mile Alaska Railroad in 1923 promised to bring new opportunities for prosperity and economic growth, Alaska was still reeling from the effects of World War 1. Men who joined the Army or went Outside to take high-paying industrial jobs often did not return to Alaska, as the post-war prosperity in the rest of the United States was simply too satisfying.

Alaska's economy was in limbo, as described in these excerpts from chapter 11 of Don Irwin's book, *The Colorful Matanuska Valley*, detailing the conditions in 1935:

"There were approximately 100 miles of graded road in the Valley in the spring of 1935. Not more than 20 miles was gravel surfaced and none of it was paved. There was no road from the Valley into Anchorage. No highway had been planned between the Valley and the Richardson Highway which runs from Valdez to Fairbanks."

The 1935 Matanuska Colony Project

The Alaska Highway, from Dawson Creek, British Columbia to Delta Junction, Alaska, would not be built for another eight years. There were no roads entering or leaving Alaska.

"Practically the only employment available to settlers in the Valley was maintenance work on the Alaska Railroad track and grade construction work with the Alaska Road Commission. A number of men were employed regularly in the gold and coal mines in the Valley and on Willow Creek."

"Both passenger and freight trains ran on the Seward to Fairbanks main line as often as the Alaska Steamship Company's boats arrived in Seward from Seattle. Usually this was on a weekly schedule during the summer months and approximately every two to three weeks during the winter months."

The passenger train took two days for the trip from Anchorage to Fairbanks, with an overnight stop at the Alaska Railroad's Curry Hotel.

"The only scheduled airline running into Anchorage in 1935 was the Star Airline operating a Ford-trimotor plane scheduling one round trip to Fairbanks each day. To fly from Anchorage to Seattle, it was necessary to go from Anchorage to Fairbanks on the Star Airline. Connections could then be made with Pan American Airways, which ran one round-trip flight per week from Seattle to Ketchikan, Juneau, Fairbanks, Nome, and return to Seattle by the same route."

Wasilla, with a population of around 100 and a general store, a roadhouse, two schools, a liquor store and a post office, was the largest town in the Valley. The town of Matanuska was half as large as Wasilla, with a general store, a hotel and a liquor store. Both towns had community centers where dances, meetings, and other events were held. There was no doctor, and no hospital facility in the Valley.

Knik had become a ghost town with the coming of the railroad, and according to Don Irwin, Palmer was comprised of one married couple and three elderly bachelors.

"As soon as news of the scheme became known, the critics and enemies of the Roosevelt administration declared the entire plan to be the wildest dream of an insane government." ~Clarence C. Hulley

Chapter Four

Roosevelt's New Deal

In America, the events of the early part of the twentieth century created what could be considered a perfect storm for social change, and that led to one of the most controversial and most widely misunderstood legacies of our 32nd President, Franklin Delano Roosevelt. His New Deal for America was a series of domestic programs enacted between 1933 and 1936 (and a few which came later), designed to transform America's economy after the stock crash of 1929 and the ensuing Great Depression.

Taking office on March 4, 1933, the jovial, optimistic, and confident Roosevelt assumed the presidency during a time of great crisis for the nation, with millions of people underemployed or unemployed. The country's industrial production had fallen dramatically, the agricultural economy was in chaos, and the banking system had become paralyzed as a widening panic drained banks of their deposits. Michigan's governor had closed all the banks in his state, and almost every state in the nation had placed some restrictions on banking activity.

On Sunday, May 7, 1933, families all across America tuned in their radios and listened as the National Broadcasting Company and the Columbia Broadcasting System aired one of President Roosevelt's avuncular Fireside Chats, titled *Outlining the New Deal Program*. In the

The 1935 Matanuska Colony Project

The tent city in Palmer, building is post office. ASL-P270-591 by Willis T. Geisman.
ARRC Album, Mary Nan Gamble Collection, Alaska State Library.

middle of his speech he described the paradox which necessitated taking unprecedented steps to bring about lasting change:

"I feel very certain that the people of this country understand and approve the broad purposes behind these new governmental policies relating to agriculture and industry and transportation. We found ourselves faced with more agricultural products than we could possibly consume ourselves and surpluses which other nations did not have the cash to buy from us except at prices ruinously low. We found our factories able to turn out more goods than we could possibly consume, and at the same time we have been faced with a falling export demand. We have found ourselves with more facilities to transport goods and crops than there were goods and crops to be transported. All of this has been caused in large part by a complete failure to understand the danger signals that have been flying ever since the close of the World War. The people of this country have been erroneously encouraged to believe that they could keep on increasing the output of farm and factory indefinitely and that some magician would find ways and means for that increased output to be consumed with reasonable profit to the producer.

"But today we have reason to believe that things are a little better than they were two months ago. Industry has picked up, railroads are carrying more freight, farm prices are better, but I am not going to indulge in issuing proclamations of over-enthusiastic assurance. We cannot ballyhoo ourselves back to prosperity. I am going to be honest at all times with the people of the country. I do not want the people of this country to take the foolish course of letting this improvement come back on another speculative wave. I do not want the people to believe that because of unjustified optimism we can resume the ruinous practice of increasing our crop output and our factory output in the hope that a kind providence will find buyers at high prices. Such a course may bring us immediate and false prosperity but it will be the kind of prosperity that will lead us into another tailspin."

During Roosevelt's first Hundred Days many acts were introduced which were to form the basis of the New Deal and cover issues of social, economic, and financial concern. By forging a coalition which included banking and oil industries, state party organizations, labor unions, farmers, blue collar workers, minorities (racial, ethnic and religious), and others, Franklin D. Roosevelt created support for his New Deal plan.

An enthusiastic, genial, but dominant leader who was swept into the Presidency in an unprecedented wave of popularity, and with the bouncy popular song *"Happy Days Are Here Again"* as his campaign theme, many of Roosevelt's acts were passed without too much scrutiny. In later years the Supreme Court declared some acts in the New Deal were unconstitutional, including the National Industrial Recovery Act, and the 1933 Agricultural Adjustment Act. But others became part of the fabric of our government, such as the Emergency Banking Act/Federal Deposit Insurance Corporation (FDIC), the Federal Securities Act of May 1933/ Securities and Exchange Commission (SEC), the National Labor Relations Act (Wagner Act), the Fair Labor Standards Act of 1938, and the Social Security Act, which established a system that provided old-age pensions for workers, survivors benefits for victims of industrial accidents, unemployment insurance, and aid for dependent mothers and children, the blind and physically disabled.

The New Deal also introduced numerous new agencies which worked with the Federal government, including the Civilian Conservation Corps (CCC), the Works Progress Administration (WPA), the Tennessee Valley Authority (TVA), the Farm Credit Administration, the Reconstruction Finance Corporation, and the Federal Emergency Relief Administration (FERA). It was this last agency which established the Matanuska Colony.

On June 25, 1934, *Time* magazine featured the charismatic but controversial agricultural economist Rexford G. Tugwell on its cover. Tugwell was one of the core of Columbia University professors who formed Franklin D. Roosevelt's infamous "Brain Trust," the academics who helped develop policy recommendations leading to Roosevelt's 1932 election as President. Tugwell subsequently served in FDR's administration, and he became the primary architect of the New Deal.

The 1935 Matanuska Colony Project

Formed under the Federal Emergency Relief Administration (FERA), the Resettlement Administration (RA) was the urbane, intellectual Rexford Tugwell's brainchild, formed to relocate struggling urban and rural families to communities planned by the federal government.

In her landmark book, *We Shall Be Remembered* (Metropolitan Press of Portland, Oregon, 1966), Evangeline Atwood, who arrived in Anchorage with her husband, Bob Atwood, publisher of the *Anchorage Times*, only a month after the Colonists arrived in Palmer, wrote about Rexford Tugwell and the Resettlement Administration:

"With nearly one hundred rural communities in the mill, Tugwell decided that the only way to keep them from decaying into rural slums would be to develop commercial agricultural units. Only through collective operation of the land could this be possible, so he decided that all farming projects should be cooperative. The RA would bring in a project manager, a farm manager, and a home supervisor who would help the settlement form consumers' cooperatives. The agency would also purchase heavy farm machinery for the community and make individual loans for operating stock."

The Matanuska Colony, Fifty Years 1935-1985 (Matanuska Impressions Printing, Palmer, Alaska 1985), by Brigitte Lively, notes that the Matanuska Colony Project was the only colony ever established in the United States. Lively also points out "...the project and the project people were celebrated and at the same time overwhelmingly criticized and condemned to failure."

The seeming paradox of concurrent celebration and condemnation underscores the incredible complexity of the project. It was an experiment, to be sure, for nothing of the magnitude or audacity had ever been attempted before, which left it wide open to all sorts of criticism and conjecture. Brigette Lively noted in her book, "From the start, the Colony had no lack of observers, critics, and experts from near and far. They all were rather uninhibited about voicing their often negative and mostly uninformed opinions."

The source of their consternation was outlined by Orlando W. Miller in his heavily-footnoted book, *The Frontier in Alaska and the Matanuska Colony* (Yale University Press, 1975):

"The Matanuska Colony was hardly more than established before confusion arose about its origins and intended purpose. In Alaska the Colony was regarded as an inept federal attempt to compensate for past neglect and to stimulate Alaskan development, and the relief and rehabilitation of rural families from depressed areas elsewhere was looked upon as a complication grafted on the plan, a perversion of what was, or should have been, the real aim–making Alaska grow."

But part of the blame could be traced directly back to the controversial Rexford G. Tugwell. Described by *Time* magazine as "top man of the Brain Trust," Tugwell believed intense planning was the key to avoiding economic and social upheaval. He was credited with statements such as: "Fundamental changes of attitude, new disciplines, revised legal structures, unaccustomed limitations on activity, are all necessary if we are to plan. This amounts, in fact, to the abandonment, finally, of laissez-faire." and "Make no small plans, for they have not the power to move men's souls."

Tugwell's plans were not small. The *Gale Encyclopedia of Biography* notes: "In some respects conservative, for he opposed welfare and believed in a balanced budget, Tugwell was intensely disliked by many opponents of the New Deal, in large measure because of his advocacy of planning, which in the 1930s was facilely associated with the type of planning carried on in the Soviet Union of Joseph Stalin.

"A suave, somewhat arrogant personality, Tugwell was readily caricatured and attracted considerable attention in the more conservative segment of the popular press as "Rex the Red, " an appellation which was not only inaccurate but painful to Tugwell. Although he was not entirely satisfied with the New Deal, regarding it as too much of a patchwork, Tugwell was willing to remain in Washington as long as he considered himself useful to the administration."

The 1935 Matanuska Colony Project

Rexford Tugwell eventually resigned due to congressional charges of socialistic and utopian leanings, but not before leaving an indelible mark on America's domestic and economic policies. He made numerous contributions to American intellectual and public life over a 60-year period, and spent many years of worthwhile public service in Puerto Rico. His scholarly writings stimulated debate over many issues, including his longtime advocacies of planning and, later, of constitutional reform.

In the northern midwest states of Michigan, Wisconsin, and Minnesota, intensive commercial lumbering practices in the late-nineteenth century left parts of the region resembling a war zone of tree stumps and forest debris.

Concerned about the future prospects of the area, the local press, merchants, and bankers promoted the area for farm settlement around the turn of the century, and between 1900 and 1920, thousands of settlers moved into the region to carve out new farms from the cut-over forest land.

A United States Department of Agriculture Bulletin, No. 425, was published on October 24, 1916, titled *Farming on the cut-over lands of Michigan, Wisconsin, and Minnesota*, authored by J. C. McDowell, Agriculturalist, and W. B. Walker, Assistant Agriculturalist. Available for five cents per copy, the introduction began:

"The cut-over district of northern Michigan, Wisconsin, and Minnesota comprises an area of about 30,000,000 acres which is rapidly being developed into farms."

After a summary of the bulletin, a description of the area followed:

"The high price of lumber in recent years has brought about the destruction of most of the pine forests in this region and has caused big inroads to be made into the forests of hardwood. Fires have also played an important part in the destruction of these northern forests. The harvesting of the crop of timber and its manufacture into lumber has made a few men very wealthy and for a long time has furnished employment to a large force of laborers at reasonably good wages.

The 1935 Matanuska Colony Project

"Strange as it may seem, the lumbermen rated the land that produced this heavy growth of timber as having little or no agricultural value. While this may be true of some of the swamp land and sandy belt areas, it is by no means generally true of this extensive cut-over district."

With photos of idyllic farms and descriptions of "the little farm well tilled," the booklet noted that "A large percentage of the settlers are foreign born. The are industrious and economical, and while their income is small, their expenses are low." and then cautioned, "Buy good land. It is cheaper in the long run than poor land."

As noted in the bulletin, the cutover settlers were often European immigrants who preferred working the land to work in America's mines and factories. Comparatively cheap prices and favorable credit terms from lumber companies–who were eager to sell land they no longer needed and didn't want to pay taxes on–allowed these families to own their farms, but as the booklet again explained, the cutover land was often rocky and covered with large tree stumps, and removing tree stumps and native rock to begin cultivation was expensive and frustrating labor.

The Great Depression wracked America in the early 1930s, leaving families destitute and men standing in breadlines. Hope was fading for thousands of Americans. Evangeline Atwood noted in her book that "...state and private welfare funds were running out. In some states forty percent of the population was on relief, and in some counties the percentage ran between eighty and ninety.

"We caseworkers were at the point were a person had to be literally dying before we could provide hospitalization. A family had to be on the verge of disaster to be eligible for relief funds. We all knew such conditions could not continue without a revolution. The one bright star on the horizon was the change which was to take place in the White House. Maybe he could come up with the answer. Certainly Herbert Hoover and his advisors appeared helpless."

The change on the horizon was, of course, Franklin D. Roosevelt.

The 1935 Matanuska Colony Project

In the late fall of 1933 and into the early months of 1934, the Federal Emergency Relief Administration (FERA) began receiving inquiries about the feasibility of sending settlers to Alaska. A report, written by FERA architect David Williams, who had become intrigued by the idea of creating a colony in the Alaskan wilderness, was circulated among relief personnel in northwestern states. Great interest was exhibited, resulting in an exploratory trip to Alaska in June, 1934, by Jacob Baker, an assistant administrator of FERA. He was escorted to the Matanuska and Tanana Valleys by Colonel O. F. Olson, Manager of the Alaska Railroad, and A. A. Shonbeck, Chairman of the Alaska Democratic Central Committee.

Back in Washington Jacob Baker reported favorably to Lawrence Westbrook, director of FERA's Division of Rural Rehabilitation, a part of Rexford Tugwell's Resettlement Administration. Orlando Miller explains what happened next in *The Frontier in Alaska and the Matanuska Colony:*

"Westbrook was impressed, requested information from the interior and agriculture departments, prepared a memorandum on a possible experimental colony for Harry Hopkins, and was later called to see Roosevelt. The president asked three questions–whether the proposed colony could support a larger population, whether the proposed colony had any military importance, and whether relief families would find the Alaskan winters endurable. Westbrook stated his conviction, based on still incomplete information, that Alaska could eventually support a larger population at a higher standard of living than all of the Scandinavian countries combined. He thought that increased agricultural production in Alaska might play an important role in supplying the troops that could eventually be stationed there. As for the northern winters, he would select settlers from Michigan, Minnesota, and Wisconsin, where the people were inured to hardships and where temperatures fell below those in the Matanuska Valley."

On February 4, 1935, Executive Order Number 5967, signed by President Roosevelt, withdrew 8,000 acres of agriculturally promising land in the eastern part of the Matanuska Valley from homestead entry. On

March 13 an additional 18,000 acres of grazing lands were withdrawn for the livestock of the Colony Project.

After that, preparations and official paperwork for the Colony Project slid into place rapidly, and Don Irwin explained what was also happening in early 1935 in his book, *The Colorful Matanuska Valley*:

"Meanwhile, in Washington, there were discussions between officials of the Department of the Interior and the FERA. It was agreed that the two organizations would undertake the Colonization Project jointly. Planning and execution of the project would be the responsibility of the FERA. The Department of Interior and the Alaska Territorial Government would cooperate fully. Funds appropriated under the Federal Emergency Relief Act of 1933 would be used to finance the project. This act gave wide authority to the FERA administrator, Harry Hopkins, to grant funds to the several states and territories to help meet the costs of hardship relief, provide work relief, and alleviate the suffering caused by unemployment.

"Early in February, 1935, solicitors acting for the FERA administrator drew up Articles of Incorporation for the Alaska Rural Rehabilitiation Corporation (ARRC). These instruments were sent, by airmail, to the Governor of Alaska in Juneau. The incorporating papers arrived at the Governor's office during the rush of the 1935 Session of the Alaska Legislature. Action on filing the incorporating papers and returning them to the FERA office in Washington was delayed until the Legislative Session adjourned early in April."

The delay created problems, but things were getting underway.

Don L. Irwin and Col. O. F. Ohlsen (right) discuss a job well done as the colonists are finally put in the tents at Palmer. ASL-P270-140 by Willis T. Geisman. ARRC Album, Mary Nan Gamble Collection, Alaska State Library.

"If the government is going to set up colonies all over the country, why not one for Alaska?" Colonel Otto F. Ohlson

Chapter Five

Laying the Groundwork

When word of the Federal Government's new program reached the press there were very mixed reactions and many misunderstandings, but the Alaskan colonization program quickly gripped the public's attention with images of brave pioneers setting forth to recreate the Manifest Destiny of their forefathers in opening new lands. This mysterious territory of Alaska was, like the frontier west before it, the stuff of legends, with towering mountains, endless forests, unknown coasts and wild uncharted rivers. But there were also captivating stories of immense glaciers, still-active volcanos, and the vast unknown expanse of the Arctic.

Reporters of the day, always on the lookout for compelling human interest stories, seemed to delight in characterizing the adventure in outrageous phrasings. The March 10, 1935 issue of the *Los Angeles Times* ran an article headlined: "Alaska Cold to Colonies: Farm Migration Held Dubious, New Deal Plan to Transport Drought-Stricken Families Viewed Askance: The Northern Lights may see such sights as a Minnesota farmer plowing Alaskan fields for rutabagas, shooting big game and catching game fish in an effort to beat the drought by a revival of the old-time American pioneer spirit."

On March 26, 1935, the *Boston Globe* purred: "Pioneers on a New Frontier: One of the experiments our Government is conducting for the relief of families stranded in the mid-West, because of the destruction of their lands, promises to stimulate attention the Nation over. There is in it just that touch of romance which lends appeal to the imagination."

And the March 24, 1935 copy of *The Washington Post* expounded: "Its Fertile Valleys Await 'Model' Group: They Will Build Log Cabins and School Houses in Region of Great Abundance, Where Vegetables Grow to Giant Size. 200 Families to Go, And 400 Laborers. Drought Areas of Michigan, Wisconsin, Minnesota Provide Population for Just Such Project in the Far North. A tent colony similar to those of the 'Klondike or Bust' days of '98 will soon greet Alaskan eyes."

Beyond the popular hype of the headlines, surveys were made on the land removed from homestead entry, the land was subdivided into 208 plots ranging from 40 to 80 acres in size, and plans were made for transporting the families to Alaska and building a new community for them; laying the groundwork for the new colony was moving ahead.

In *Matanuska Valley Memoir*, Johnson and Stanton explained the formation of the Alaska Rural Rehabilitation Corporation (ARRC), aka the Corporation in the official paperwork, which would be charged with managing the new colony:

"Direction of the Colony was to be the function of the ARRC, better known as the Corporation. The AARC was incorporated on April 12, 1935 under the Alaskan laws relating to charitable agencies. It was to be a non-profit corporation, given broad powers to operate anywhere in Alaska for no longer than fifty years. The Articles of Incorporation were drawn up from a standard form used for the incorporation of Rural Rehabilitation Corporations in the United States.

"The primary purpose for which the Corporation was formed is stated to be 'To rehabilitate individuals and families as self-sustaining human beings by enabling them to secure subsistence and gainful employment from the soil, from coordinate and affiliated industries and enterprises or otherwise, in accordance with economic and social standards of good citizenship.'

"Eleven other objects and purposes in the Articles defined specific powers by which the corporation was to accomplish its primary objectives. Express provision was made that the statements shall not be considered to restrict the Corporation's power in any manner."

In the general elections of November, 1932, the Senate had gained a Democratic majority of over two to one, while the House came out of the elections with a three to one Democratic majority. President Herbert Hoover famously said the 1932 election had not been a "contest between two men" but one between "two philosophies of government."

The stage was set for major change.

In 2009 *Time* magazine published *"The Legacy of F.D.R,"* which capsulized one of the most notable eras in American history, beginning with the new President Roosevelt's taking office:

"March 4, 1933, was perhaps the Great Depression's darkest hour. The stock market had plunged 85% from its high in 1929, and nearly one-fourth of the workforce was unemployed. In the cities, jobless men were lining up for soup and bread. In rural areas, farmers whose land was being foreclosed were talking openly of revolution. The crowd that gathered in front of the Capitol that day to watch Franklin D. Roosevelt's Inauguration had all but given up on America. They were, a reporter observed, "as silent as a group of mourners around a grave."

"Roosevelt's Inaugural Address was a pitch-perfect combination of optimism ('The only thing we have to fear is fear itself'), consolation (the nation's problems 'concern, thank God, only material things') and resolve ('This nation asks for action, and action now'). The speech won rave reviews. Even the rock-ribbed Republican *Chicago Tribune* lauded its 'dominant note of courageous confidence.' F.D.R. had buoyed the spirits of the American people — and nearly 500,000 of them wrote to him at the White House in the following week to tell him so.

"Hours after the Inauguration, Roosevelt made history in a more behind-the-scenes way. He gathered his Cabinet in his White House office and had Justice Benjamin Cardozo swear them in as a group, the first time that had ever been done. F.D.R. joked that he was doing it so they could 'receive an extra day's pay,' but the real reason was that he wanted his team to get to work immediately.

"And that team came through brilliantly. In the next 100 days — O.K., 105, but who's counting? — his Administration shepherded 15 major bills through Congress. It was the most intense period of lawmaking ever undertaken by Congress — a 'presidential barrage of ideas and programs,' historian Arthur Schlesinger Jr. observed, 'unlike anything known to American history.'"

When the seventy-third United States Congress convened under the new Roosevelt administration in 1933, the federal bureaucracy was fairly small, and concerned itself primarily with overseeing relatively minor regulations on various growing industries.

The federal government's role in times of economic crisis had traditionally been to offer loans to state governments through the Emergency Relief Administration (ERA), so they could tend to the welfare of their citizens. But with the Great Depression wreaking havoc across the nation, 15 million Americans were unemployed, and their first order of business became working with the administration to draft a program to aid the millions of Americans displaced by the unprecedented hardships of the times.

The Federal Emergency Relief Act of 1933, a joint federal-state relief effort, replaced the Emergency Relief Administration with an appropriation of $500 million dollars set aside for the relief effort; $250 million of that was designated for use by the states "to make grants to the several states to aid in meeting the costs of furnishing relief and in relieving the hardship and suffering caused by unemployment in the form of money, service, materials, and/or commodities to provide the necessities of life to persons in need as a result of the present emergency, and/or their dependents, whether resident, transient, or homeless," as well as to "aid in assisting cooperative and self-help associations for the barter of goods and services."

The 1935 Matanuska Colony Project

To facilitate the administration of this new emergency relief program, the Federal Emergency Relief Administration (FERA) established a State Emergency Relief Administration (SERA) in each state, but officials quickly learned that the rural areas were not interested in a relief program as much as a rehabilitation program.

In April, 1934, a Rural Rehabilitation Division was established within FERA, with funds designated for use only in rural areas. Rural relief camps were established across the nation, to give families a place to stay until times improved; in time they would be immortalized by the great documentary photographer Dorothea Lange, and in John Steinbeck's epic masterpiece, *The Grapes of Wrath*.

In order to effectively assist the people who needed it, however, the states needed the power to handle a myriad of additional functions relative to a diversified rural rehabilitation effort, so FERA authorized the establishment of legal entities in each of the states: not-for-profit organizations known as rural rehabilitation corporations which would allow each state to craft rehabilitation programs that met their own needs. By 1935, forty-five rural rehabilitation corporations were formed, with similar corporations in the territories of Alaska, Hawaii, and Puerto Rico.

The corporations began to buy huge tracts of farmland, subdivided them into homestead plots, and mortgaged the plots to displaced farm families. In addition to the Matanuska Colony at Palmer, FERA completed three other communities: Dyess Colony, Arkansas; Cherry Lake, Florida; and Pine Mountain Valley Resettlement Community, Georgia.

Over time, nearly 200 communities, including Arthurdale, West Virginia; Greenbelt, Maryland; Farmstead, Alabama; Greendale, Wisconsin; Cumberland Homesteads, Tennessee; and Greenhills, Ohio, would reap the benefits of what came to be known as the federal government's 'alphabet agencies.'

David Reichard Williams, born a twin in his parents' sod house in Childress, Texas, in 1890, grew up mostly educated at home and through correspondence courses. He started to work for the Fort Worth and Denver City Railway System when he was only 15. At the age of 22 he began a study of architecture at the University of Texas, and in 1916, without having received a degree, he accepted a job as a civil engineer for Gulf Oil Corporation in Mexico, gaining an appreciation for Spanish Colonial architecture while there. He also designed a simple system of pre-fabrication which was adopted by the oil companies and used world-wide; he later became a recognized expert in the field of prefabricated buildings, and he would use the concept in the Matanuska Colony Project.

Williams spent 1922 and 1923 in Europe, and his extensive travels there, along with his exposure to the modern masters, would later influence his work designing distinctive homes which drew upon the tenets of European Modernism, while also incorporating many inspirations from the handcrafted work of early Texas pioneers.

Williams' goal was to do for Texas what Frank Lloyd Wright had done for the Midwest with his Prairie style home; that is, to design a sturdy, functional type of home, designed to meet regional needs. His successful Texas Modernist style, exhibiting a respect for the environment, an ability to adapt to a region, and a tradition of craftsmanship, was adopted by many other architects, and his development of an indigenous architecture for the American southwest would later lead to the popular "ranch house" home design.

In 1933 David Williams developed the first large-scale community building project in the United States, the Woodlake Cooperative Agricultural Community in east Texas. Designed to give depression-era families an opportunity to become farmers, the project was deemed a great success by supporters of the New Deal, and in 1934 Williams was called to Washington, D.C. to work with FERA, planning agricultural communities.

After researching Alaska's climate and agricultural potential, requesting information from the Arctic Institute of North America and the University of Minnesota, and interviewing Alaskan construction experts, Williams wrote up guidelines and a proposal, and he and others met with President Roosevelt in February 1935 to propose the Matanuska Colony

Project. Roosevelt was strongly in favor of developing an Alaskan farming community which could supply future Alaskan military bases, and the project was given a green light. David Williams was directed to finalize plans for the new Alaskan community.

Williams oversaw the design of indigenous log and frame buildings, utilizing his concepts of pre-fabrication to orchestrate the pre-cutting of logs for homes, barns, and outbuildings. The first summer was dedicated to building the Colonists' houses, which were available in five designs. As a measure of expediency Williams only designed one barn, a distinctive structure with a high gambrel roof, measuring 32 feet by 32 feet square, and 32 feet high. The barns were built on small pilings of native spruce, the spruce logs sawn flat on three sides making up the ten foot high log side walls. Above that was wood siding up to the frame-constructed gambrel roof. Outbuildings were also designed, and included a chicken coop/brooder with a shed roof, a well house and an outhouse.

Having never been to Alaska, Williams was not aware that the local trees in some areas were too small for effective sawmilling into useable lumber, so in the summer of 1935 he would travel north to troubleshoot construction problems.

In the April 13, 1935 issue of the *Ironwood Daily News*, Ironwood, Michigan, the following article appeared under the heading "Alaskan Expedition to be Led by Wyoming Rancher:"

"Washington, April 13--(AP)--A lean and bronzed Wyoming rancher is in Washington preparing to lead a new-style pioneering expedition into an Alaskan valley late this month.

"He is D.L. Irwin and his title is 'director of colonization for Alaska for the federal emergency relief administration.' The fertile Matanuska valley, 125 miles north of Seward, has been selected as the site for the first FERA rehabilitation colony in Alaska.

"Under consideration for several months, the project has attracted attention of the American Red Cross. Chairman Cary T. Grayson announced today that first aid training will be given the 480 relief workers who will spend the summer helping build the colony. They will receive the training before the first contingent sails from California April 20.

"Admiral Grayson added that a Red Cross public health nurse will be assigned to the colony for a year to serve as a visiting nurse and to teach home hygiene, while the junior Red Cross is assembling a library for both children and adults.

"Two hundred families--including 1,000 persons--have been selected from farms in northern Minnesota, Michigan and Wisconsin to form the colony. Each family will be lent $3,000 and will be furnished a 40-acre homestead. Thirty years will be allowed for repayment of the money. The 480 relief workers who help launch the project will return to the states in the fall, leaving the farmers to carry on.

"Irwin is tall, slightly stooped. His face is weather-beaten. Crow's feet at the corners of his eyes bear out his statement that he has spent most of his life outdoors.

"Early in 1934, he explained, efforts were begun to get him to leave his ranch to assume charge of the government experiment station in Matanuska valley. He took his wife, two daughters and young son and went there in June, 1934. In January of this year, he was summoned to Washington and told he was to take charge of the colonization project.

"Of pioneering stock, Irwin's eyes glow as he talks about the venture. He likes Alaska - America's 'last frontier.' 'I think Alaska is one of the few spots in the world where there is a future,' he said, simply.

"The colonists should succeed, he said. They will be located within a seven-mile radius of a community center. They must build their own homes and they must clear their own ground. They will be able to kill some small game for food. They will have excellent fishing. It is truly a pioneering expedition, he said--but the government will help take the raw edge off the venture. There will be portable sawmills, tractors and thousands of pounds of equipment.

"'It's a great country,' Irwin said. 'My family is still up there, you know, and we'll have to build our home like the rest of them.

"'I'll be glad to get back.'"

In his book, *The Frontier in Alaska and the Matanuska Colony,* Orlando Miller commented about an interview he had with Irwin: "To his disappointment, he was assigned to planning for supplies and shipments rather than given authority to select the colonists, a job he would have preferred and believed he could have done well."

Irwin had begun methodically determining standards to apply to the colonist selection process, but his approach was deemed too slow and he was rejected in favor of a committee determining the selection process. Irwin found himself planning the initial procuring and transportation of building materials, construction and farm equipment, and livestock for the colony. He would later write in *The Colorful Matanuska Valley*:

"This was no light order. Two ships–a troop carrier, the St. Mihiel, and a Bureau of Indian Affairs supply ship, the North Star–were chartered for $50,000 and put into commission for a period of six months. These two ships transported the Colonists, transient workers, equipment, material and supplies necessary for the operation of the project for the first six months.

"Transportation of approximately 1,000 people from their home-counties to the state concentration points and thence across the states to San Francisco by train, was only part of the problem. Feeding them and providing for sleeping and sanitation were more complex. There was criticism of the accommodations by those who opposed the plan. Colonel Ohlson had been in public service long enough to let the critics find fault. He had work to do, and he went about the job in hand, always two jumps ahead of the politicians and fault finders. Many of the ideas of the planners in Washington were obviously out of line with the hard facts and conditions in Alaska."

Irwin's last line was a point which would be heard often in the months and years ahead.

"Only honest-to-God, hardy, pioneer-type farmers are to be considered." Colonel Lawrence Westbrook

Chapter Six

Selecting Families

A third-generation Alaskan born in Sitka in 1906, Maud "Evangeline" Rasmuson was the daughter of Alaskan banker E. A. Rasmuson. As a social worker in Springfield, Illinois in the early 1930's, she met and married Robert Atwood. Returning to Alaska at the same time as the Colonists were settling into their tents in Palmer, the Atwoods enlisted the aid of Evangeline's father, E. A. Rasmuson, and purchased *The Anchorage Daily Times*, which had been founded in May, 1915, and had at the time, 650 subscribers. That was over 30 percent of the population of Anchorage, which at that time was a mere 2,200 people.

Evangeline Atwood became an important figure in the fight for Alaskan statehood. She wrote several books on Alaska politics and history, and was very active in Anchorage and Alaskan civic affairs. Her 1966 book, *We Shall Be Remembered*, is one of the handful of books which reliably chronicled the Colony Project, and Evangeline Atwood's experience as a social worker in the very decade which spawned the Project gave her valuable insight and empathy. She wrote:

"It was no easy task for the social workers to say no to this family, and yes to another, when so many had come to the end of their rope and could see nothing in the future for themselves and their children. The workers

Waiting to be assigned to tents. ASL-P270-136 by Willis T. Geisman.
ARRC Album, Mary Nan Gamble Collection, Alaska State Library.

did not realize at the beginning that there would be such an urge to go to faraway, rugged Alaska. But also they had not realized how hopeless and desperate life had become to so many who were still struggling to stay off the relief rolls.

"The idea of starting a new life in a distant place like Alaska was so appealing to the disheartened that the workers found it difficult to determine which ones really were equipped to make the drastic move and which ones were simply motivated by wishful thinking. They reminded themselves of the bases for selection as laid down in the planning sessions in Washington:

"Couples must be physically strong and mentally ambitious and be possessed of a rugged, pioneering spirit. No particular attention should be paid to a group of related families, or racial or religious factors, excepting that the group should be basically of the Nordic type and fitted by living habits to adjust to the Alaska environment. The entire group must be selected on a basis to cooperate in a commercial enterprise.

"As far as possible, families should be selected first on their farming ability and secondly, those who may have secondary skills and who may adjust themselves to a diversified farming activity and can assist with carpentry on their homes and then those who may know something about machinery and blacksmithing and who have leadership qualities."

One key to understanding how the selection process–as described in the last paragraph–was developed, can be found in an article by Arnold R. Alanen, emeritus professor in the Department of Landscape Architecture, University of Wisconsin, for *Perspectives in Vernacular Architecture*, Volume 8 in the series from the University of Tennessee Press titled *People, Power, Places* (2000).

Alanen's article, *Midwesterners in the Matanuska Valley: Colonizing Rural Alaska during the 1930s*, noted:

"There was, however, an important difference between two groups of individuals involved in promoting and planning the Matanuska settlement. One group, typified by Westbrook and M. D. Snodgrass, manager of the agricultural experiment station in Palmer, believed that Alaska's environmental and economic constraints would never allow the colonists' farms to proceed beyond a subsistence level; therefore, they felt that individuals with skills in fields such as carpentry and blacksmithing could pursue small-scale, part-time farming for supplementary income. On the other hand, architect Williams, the media, and some Alaskan officials and boosters claimed that the colonists could develop profitable dairy farms and sell their excess produce to the territory's future settlers and residents."

As it happened, both points of view were represented in the final analysis, and individuals of both persuasions were later evident in the Colony Project. This disparity of attitudes was complicated by the fact that the Project was never intended to produce a community of self-sufficient farmers. An excess of farm production, spurred by the developments of motorized farm machinery, electrification, and mass production methods, had contributed to the perfect storm which became the Great Depression. Orlando Miller noted that "...the resettlement program was not intended to invite disaster by increasing markedly the nation's supply of good farms and skilled farmers."

While this might seem incongruent with modern perceptions of rugged pioneers setting forth to conquer the wilderness, that was not, in fact, the goal of the planners. Miller explains:

"The 'real farmers,' who according to critics should have been chosen for the Matanuska project, were found only rarely in backwoods America. Journalists and others, influenced by received ideas about the pioneer past, regularly praised the pioneer character and found it little in evidence in the colony. However, what they saw among the colonists–the careless methods, the fondness for endlessly unresolved bickerings, the suspicion of expert advice or authority–perhaps resulted less from the disappearance of the frontier character than from its spotty persistence. FERA officials and others concerned with rural poverty and resettlement often made ceremonial references to the frontier and pioneers, but their problem was the reduction of relief rolls and the rehabilitation of rural families."

The 1935 Matanuska Colony Project

Arnold Alanen's article described the route planners took to define the process of selection:

"In March 1935, representatives from relief agencies in the three states were called to Washington, where they received information about the envisioned project from Westbrook and other FERA officials. The assembled representatives were informed that they should coordinate the selection of two hundred families, giving consideration only to 'honest-to-God' farmers and 'families who love the soil.' Inquiries by 'fly-by-nights, weaklings or curious folks' were to be discouraged. County social workers were then charged with the task of developing a pool of possible applicants, with the names being forwarded to the state office for final selection. Detailed procedures were adopted to judge the families 'from the standpoint of relief eligibility, health, ability to fit into a cooperative enterprise of this nature, initiative and resourcefulness, credit rating of the family before the depression, school records of all the children and special talents of members of the family.'"

The ARRC forms and records of the Matanuska Colony Project, maintained in the National Archives in Anchorage, tell the stories of the families who were selected in stark black and white, and show the extent to which the potential families were grilled and scrutinized by the caseworkers. The names of the individuals have been omitted, as I've chosen to respect the privacy of the families, but I've tried to replicate the forms as closely as possible, and no words have been changed from what appears on the original paperwork.

ALASKA RURAL REHABILITATION CORPORATION

-o0o-

MATANUSKA VALEY SETTLEMENT AGREEMENT

THIS AGREEMENT made this _____ day of _____, 1935, between the ALASKA RURAL REHABILITATION CORPORATION, whose principal office is at Juneau, Alaska, hereinafter known as the Corporation, and __________, of the county of __________, State of Michigan, whose Post Office address is __________, hereinafter known as the Colonist, in behalf of himself and family, consisting of the following members: ____________________, W I T N E S S E T H, that

The 1935 Matanuska Colony Project

WHEREAS the Colonist and his family desire to settle on tillable land in the Matanuska Valley in the Territory of Alaska in order to obtain subsistence and gainful employment from the soil and coordinated enterprises, establish a home, and enjoy the benefits of the Rural Community now being formed there; and

WHEREAS the Corporation is a non-profit organization and has been organized and established to assist worthy and well-qualified individuals and families to accomplish the above mentioned purposes and it desires to assist the Colonist and the members of his family in doing so;

THEREFORE BE IT AGREED, for and in consideration of the above premises and the mutual covenants herein contained, as follows:

1. TRANSPORTATION TO ALASKA

The Corporation will assume the obligation to the transportation companies of the freight transportation of household and other effects up to two thousand (2,000) pounds of the Colonist and the above mentioned members of his family from the point of departure to Palmer Station in the Matanuska Valley, and advance and pay for the purchase of, and include in said freight and its transportation, such needed household furniture, small tools and home equipment as shall be agreed upon; some to be ultimately repaid by the Colonist at the same low cost and special Colonist rates as that charged by the Corporation.*

*The expense of travel of the Colonist and the members of his family and the carriage of their baggage from the point of departure to destination in Alaska is to be attended by the Emergency Relief Administration of the home state at no cost to the Colonist or members of his family and with no obligation of repayment.

2. TEMPORARY CARE

Upon arrival of the Colonist and his family at the Palmer Station the Corporation will make available tents for their temporary shelter and habitation pending construction of their dwelling house and their moving on the land which they expect to make their permanent home.

3. LAND AND HOME IN THE RURAL COMMUNITY

The Corporation will make available to the Colonist for a farm and home for himself and his family not less than forty (40) acres of land on terms of payment running over a period of thirty years.**

The Corporation will finance the Colonist in building his dwelling house and other permanent improvements on the land. The Colonist will repay for the same on an amortized plan over a period of thirty years.

**The Corporation is in a position to make available to the Colonists timbered land as low as Five ($5.00) Dollars an acre and other land at prices in proportion thereto depending upon the location and the extent to which the land has been cleared.

4. FARM MACHINERY AND EQUIPMENT

The Corporation will furnish the Colonist farm machinery, equipment, livestock and other supplies and furnishings on such use-charge, lease, rental or sale as may be agreed upon.

5. SUBSISTENCE

The Corporation will furnish subsistence to the Colonist and the above members of his family at actual cost from their arrival at Palmer Station until such time as the products which the Colonist and his family raise will enable him directly or by exchange or sale to furnish subsistence for himself and his family.

6. COMMUNITY ACTIVITIES

The Corporation will build and equip such educational, cultural, recreational, health, work, and business centers in the community as the life of the community shall require, and make the same available to the Colonist and members of his family and other members of the community, and will furnish social and economic direction, supervisory and consultation services to the Colonist, members of his family and other members of the community on terms of mutual agreement and accord.

FULFILLMENT OF THIS AGREEMENT

The Colonist agrees that the relationship established by this contract between him and the Corporation is to assist him and the members of his family to become established in a new home on a self-sustaining and self-supporting basis, and that he will repay all loans made to him by the Corporation in connection with the provisions under the above numbered headings of this agreement or otherwise made to him by the Corporation, and pay for all materials, supplies, equipment, furnishings, services, and personal, real, or mixed property referred to in the provisions under the above numbered headings of this agreement or otherwise furnished him by the Corporation, which are rented, leased, or sold to him by or through the Corporation, upon such terms as are agreed upon, and will enter into and perform all obligations and contracts necessary in order to do so; it being understood that interest rates on all obligations shall not be greater than three (3) per cent per annum from the time they are incurred and that payment of said interest shall not begin until the first day of September, 1938, and that payment of installments of the principal on all said obligations shall not begin until the first day of September, 1940, unless the Colonist elects to make such payments at an earlier date.

The Colonist further agrees that he and the members of his family will abide by all Corporation administrative directions and supervision in connection with control of crop production, processing, marketing, distribution, crop rotation, soil management, sanitation and other measures for the welfare of the community, and to cooperate with the Corporation, its representatives, and with the other Colonists in building up a successful Rural Community.

It is mutually agreed by the parties hereto that this agreement is subject to any Federal, State, or Territorial laws now existing or which may be hereafter enacted.

ALASKA RURAL REHABILITATION CORPORATION

BY ____________________ ____________________
(Name) (Title)

____
(The Colonist)

WITNESSES

____

____

....

SOCIAL HISTORY SHEET

Case #____
Name of Colonist and wife
Address of Colonist

SOURCE
Special investigation of this family as they have expressed themselves as being particularly interested in the World Alaska Rehabilitation Project.

DIRECTIONS FOR REACHING HOME
A detailed description of how to locate the family's home. "Large elm tree in front of house and cobble stone part pillars on porch."

DATE OF HOME VISIT
April 6, 1935
Contacted all three members of this family: Man, Wife, and Daughter (child of W by first marriage). All members were immediately neat, clean, and dressed in good taste. M was dressed in sports clothes consisting of breeches, high boots, and sweater. He has a splendid carriage, is most congenial, has a good face and could even be called good looking. His complexion is ruddy and he is the perfect picture of health. One would call him the typical out-door man. He uses very He uses very good English and speaks with confidence. One is immediately impressed with the idea that he is a fairly well read person. He has travelled considerably and is able to discuss places, climates, and peoples with ease. W greeted visitor most courteously and appeared to be well versed in

hospitality. She is not as rugged looking as her husband, but nevertheless is in good health, enjoys out-door life and seems to be an agreeable person. M and W treated each other with the utmost respect. D, age 12, is a sweet, self conscious school girl with a nice smile and polite manners.

LEGAL SETTLEMENT

Having been residents of (county name) since 1930 and without relief until December 2, 1933, he is a legal resident of (county name). They moved to their present location in January 1933.

HOME

This small farm is worked on shares and is really on the edge of (city name). M's sister owns this place and she has asked him to vacate as soon as possible so that she can move in. House has seven rooms all furnished but this family own only part of the furniture. In fact, they only own one stove which is small but in good shape and has an oven as part of the chimney arrangement. This makes a good heater as well as an excellent cooker and baker. Six dining chairs, one leather rocker, one wooden rocker, small kitchen cabinet, some dishes, one copper boiler, tubs, kitchen utensils, few books and about 300 lbs. of tools. House looked neat and clean and liveable in all respects.

PERSONAL HISTORY OF M

M was born in (city and county name) in December of 1891. At the time of his birth his father had his own business which was that of running a livery stable. He did this for ten years and he also was Post Master of (city) for 16 years. The first (family name) came from France during the French Revolution and they settled in Hornellsville, New York. When the family first came to Michigan, M's father was partner in a lumber business. M's mother is still living and she has been making her home with this son. The agreement was that he would inherit a forty acre tract that she owned if he took care of her in her last days. She has been with them for the past three years. Her mind is gradually weakening since she had a partial stroke some years ago and she has become quite a care. The other brothers will take care of her if other plans are made for M and his family.

The mother had considerable musical talent and gave piano lessons in her younger days. This son inherited his mother's love for music and a fair singing voice. He used to play the cello but has not touched one for a number of years. M's father died in 1924 at the age of 70, but believe cause to have been senility. M attended school in (city) and finished 10th grade. At age of 9, he accompanied his mother when she spent the winter months in Phoenix, Arizona, visiting people who lived there. Even though he was a youngster the wide open spaces appealed to him and made a lasting impression. His father was anxious for his children to get a good education. He, himself, had a business education and he was eager for his children to get more schooling than he had the opportunity to get. He was a stern man but kindly to his family. In 1912, M married in (city name). From this union there were three children, two of whom are dead. One child, a boy, is living with the mother. They were divorced in 1928 after a rather unhappy married life.

The 1935 Matanuska Colony Project

PERSONAL HISTORY OF W

W was born in Manitowoc, Wisconsin in 1895. Her parents were (names). They are both alive but are divorced and remarried. Her mother lives in Detroit and her father in Pennsylvania. W finished ninth grade in Manitowoc and then took a course in sewing. Parents encouraged their children to remain in school but could not win their point with child. She continued to live in this town until she reached the age of 19. W's first husband was (name) from whom she got a divorce in 1927. In 1929 she married (husband) in Toledo, Ohio and they have been very happy together.

CHILDREN

D, only child of W by her first marriage, was born in Manitowoc, Wis. in 1922. She is now in the 6th grade being an only average student. She is very fond of out door sports, is in excellent health and has only had chicken pox to mar her health record.

RELATIVES

Blanche, sister of M died at age 19 of some female ailment.

Floyd, brother of M died in February 1935 at age of 56 of heart trouble, no doubt due to pressure on heart from chronic stomach trouble and gas that had given him considerable worry previously.

Loyal E. (address). Married and with 4 children. Works at Chevrolet Gear and Axle Co., Detroit.

Earl (address). Married and has three children. In business with brother Bert.

Bert (address). Married but has no children. Their business is in the (name and address of company).

HEALTH

All in excellent health, no drunkards as far as can be determined. No insanity and no TB. M's eyes seem to be in good condition but he has a droopy right eye lid.

RECREATION AND RELIGION

Do not attend church and are not members of any church. M is a third degree mason having joined in Bear Lake, Michigan. His dues are ten years in arrears. M is a great reader and enjoys good books especially biographies. W and daughter also like to read. One of the main questions asked by W was "Will there be a library there where good books will be available?" Chess is their favorite game and they manage to spend many a quiet evening around the board.

EMPLOYMENT HISTORY OF W

W had only a few odd jobs clerking but she worked in an ice cream parlor for years before her first marriage.

EMPLOYMENT HISTORY OF M

For five years after leaving school, M worked for his father on his forty acre tract. As renumeration he gave his son room and board and then in 1910 he gave him his second trip to Arizona where he visited for six months. Having visited there in 1900 with his mother, he had a hankering to return as the call of the west had gotten under his skin. From 1912 until 1915 M was employed at the T. B. Eggyl Hardware Store in Detroit, demonstrating and repairing tractors. He had one and a half year's experience with the General Motors Central Forge Shop in Detroit, in the tool and die department. His wages were cut on this job so M went farming at Bear Lake, Manistee County and was there for four years. In 1928, M spent six months in California visiting with relatives. One uncle is a professor in the University of Southern California (USC) in Los Angeles. After returning, M accepted a job with the Brantner Heating Engineer Co. of Detroit as installer and repair man on steam and warm air. During his second year with this concern, he was salesman, returning to (city) in 1930. Since this time M has worked for various farmers for shares and has a good farming record and is held in high esteem in his own town. He loves the land and has been happiest when working on farms. He does not care to ever return to any city and both he and his wife long for the wide open spaces.

FINANCES

M had his life insured with the Mutual Benefit Life Insurance Co. of Newark, N.J. but dropped the policy in 1930 when it became impossible to pay the premiums. Had a savings account in a Detroit bank but has had none since 1930. Very few debts: $4.50 to Atwood Shaeffer Battery and Tire Shop for a battery, $3.24 to Northern Service Auto Co. for transmission work on car, $5.50 to Dr. Parsons for dental work, $10 to Jerome Cole for rent of cow for one year, sold his Dodge Commercial Truck in February for $60 to take care of some pressing debts. Creditors are not pressing now but M states that he can settle up all debts before departing for the north country.

SOCIAL PROBLEMS

Family seems to be happy, optimistic and cheerful over their reverses, but are most eager to make this real change for they feel there is much to gain and nothing to lose. W is just as anxious as M to take the step.

RECOMMENDATIONS

After discussing at length all these matters with this family, I recommend that this family be given serious consideration for the Alaskan Rehabilitation Project. The only thing that might be an exception is the man's age, which is 42, but being unusually strong and robust, it would seem that this matter would enter in as an exception.

Lela M. Rahm, Case Supervisor
(COUNTY NAME) EMERGENCY RELIEF COMMISSION

....

RELIEF INVESTIGATION

Name (Colonist) — Case. No ___
Address — Caseworker Mr. Westoff

I. Application

The 1935 Matanuska Colony Project

A. General Information

1. Applied March 25, 1935
2. (Name) made application personally.
3. Applied for relief as he was unable to find employment.
4. Application taken by Miss Wensing.

II. (Name) was interviewed at home on March 26th.

A. Description of Members of Family, Home, Property

1. Individuals

The family consists of the husband, wife, and one child. The type of clothing worn by the family is comfortable and warm. They seem to get along very well.

2. Home

They live in a four-room cottage that is clean and very well kept. There are ample sleeping quarters with plenty of bedding. The cottage is lighted by kerosene lamps. The wife seems to be a very capable housekeeper. Did not notice any reading material.

3. Property

The property belongs to (name and address). This man is retained as care taker with no salary. However, he receives the increase from the cows and has ample acreage for raising his own vegetables and a place for a garden. At the present time there are no milk checks.

B. Residence

1. (Name) came from Chicago in 1932. Before coming here he worked for different factories, the last one being the Louis Hansen Co.. He has always worked as a common laborer. In the years of 1930 and 1931 his weekly wages averaged $20.00.

2. (Name) left Chicago because he could not find further employment.

3. His legal residence is in (name of county).

C. War History

None.

D. Religion

None.

E. Race and Nationality

1. The client was born in Germany. He is now a citizen of the U.S.

2. He received his first papers in 1927, his second in 1934.

3. Client claims he is not interested in what is going on in Germany. He is happy he came to America, and has adopted our customs and manner of living.

F. Relatives

There seem to be no relatives on either side of the family, except those remaining in Germany.

G. Health

The health of the entire family is very good.

H. Employment - Other than relief

(Name) has always worked as a common laborer on construction jobs.

I. Education

(Names) completed the 9th grade in school.

J. Recreation

The family live beside the Menoninee River where there is boating, swimming and fishing in the summer season.

K. Delinquency

None.

L. Marital Relations

The family get along well together.

M. Debts

None.

••••••••••••••••••••••••••••••

Stories of many of the selected Colony families have been told by previous authors, of course, and the stories shared are quite compelling, detailing the often hard–but sometimes easy–decisions which were made.

In *Matanuska Colony, Fifty Years: 1935-1985*, Brigitte Lively told of Johan Johanson, who "saw all his corn and other standing crops blown down by a storm one day. The next day, a freeze killed all his vegetables. The third day fire destroyed his home. He told a reporter then, 'It was the depression more than the drought. After the place was ruined, I couldn't get work and was pretty desperate.'"

Evangeline Atwood wrote about Larry Vasanoja, who was working in the county welfare office in Cloquet, Minnesota:

"His supervisor came over to his desk one morning and said: 'Mr. Vasanoja, I want you to pick out nine families whom you think could go to Alaska and make successful farmers.'

"Larry's eyes opened wide and he asked, 'Can I choose myself?' Assured that he could, he picked up the phone and called his next-door neighbor, Loren McKechnie, and asked if he wanted to come along. Sure he did. They talked with their wives, and both Helen and Edna were so excited about the idea that they grabbed each other around the waist and began dancing in the middle of the living room, chanting 'We're going to Alaska! We're going to Alaska!'

"Larry also invited Virgil Eckert, another friend, to join the Alaska party. The Vasanojas had five children, the Eckerts two, and the McKechnies five."

In his article *Midwesterners in the Matanuska Valley: Colonizing Rural Alaska during the 1930s*, Professor Arnold Alanen wrote:

"Oscar Kertulla of Deer River, Minnesota, expressed both stoicism and hope as he, his wife, Elvi, and their son and daughter set off for Alaska: 'Nothing can discourage us now,' he wrote in his diary. 'The worst has happened that could possibly happen to us. Cattle have died, farms are ruined, dust storms and blizzards have left us little in material wealth; all that is left to us is courage to try and carve new homes for ourselves in the North.'"

Newspapers of the day found heart-wrenching human interest stories for their readers, such as this report in the *Ironwood Daily Globe*, in Ironwood, Michigan, headlined 'Families Pack Up for Alaska,' dated May 6, 1935, and sent over the wires of the Associated Press:

"Rhinelander, May 6--(AP)--Fired with the zeal of early American colonists, some with adventure, others with independence as their goal, 67 families from the wastelands of Wisconsin today were packing for their journey to the fertile fields of Alaska's Matanuska Valley.

The 1935 Matanuska Colony Project

"The 317 men, women, and children of the Badger branch of the government's new FERA colony will leave from here, Superior, Green Bay and St. Paul by train this weekend for Seattle where they will embark on the sea leg of the trip.

"Grimly, they have prepared for the hardships that were predicted. The Alaskan picture was not painted too bright, lest some fancy a new paradise after harrowing years here.

"Those who have felt the sting of Wisconsin's bitter blizzards or the blaze of the summer sun on parched scrublands wonder if Alaska with all its rough climate and unsettled frontiers can make earning a livlihood more difficult than it has been here.

"The Martin Soyks of Minoqua, for instance. The demands of a paradise are small after their years here.

"'We're going to Alaska,' said Mrs. Soyk with an inflection of thrilled awe in her voice. Typical of the women of the group is this mere strip of a girl whose countenance worry has marked with the lines that to most others come with age.

"'We're going through with it, all the way, we're enthusiastic about it. I think I'll have a better opportunity to make a living. Here our place isn't big enough.'

"The 'place' was a shack that Soyk had piled together after one of the misfortunes in a long series befell them. It stood on the clearing Soyk bought after their marriage.

"Once it had a fine long cottage, built by Soyk, a natural born carpenter. There the young mother cared for her first born, Sonny. When the second lad, Jimmie, was born not long after Sonny, the mother grew seriously ill. Sonny became ill and died.

"One day the three were out in the surrounding section and saw smoke from what they believed was a haystack near their home. They returned to find their log cottage and all their belongings in ashes.

"'All we had left,' Mrs. Soyk said, 'was the clothes on our backs. This place here is just a shack that Martin threw together so we'd have something.'

"Living in Alaska, she said, is 'going to be hard work,' but she said she felt cheered by the knowledge that some of their neighbors envy them.

"With slight variations, Mrs. Soyk's story tells that of most others of the group. Some ask only adventure, but the Soyks and others will take thrills as garnish for the fruits of toil they found unproductive here."

Mothers and babies arriving at the Matanuska train station. ASL-P270-225
by Willis T. Geisman. ARRC Album, Mary Nan Gamble Collection, Alaska State Library.

"Alaska is about the only unsettled country we have left." ~Harry L Hopkins

Chapter Seven

Bound for Alaska

On March 14, 1935, Colonel Lawrence Westbrook, an engineer, agriculturalist, and director of FERA's Division of Rural Rehabilitation, called social workers from Minnesota, Michigan, and Wisconsin to a meeting in Washington, D.C., where planning sessions were laid out and criteria explained for selection of the settler families. The Minnesota contingent of the Colonist families would be traveling west to depart from San Francisco, while the families from Wisconsin and Michigan would board the ship at Seattle two weeks later, in an effort to mollify the Seattle businessmen who complained that the San Francisco stores and businesses were reaping all the financial rewards of supplying the Colony.

As the social workers returned home to their respective states and set about their task of screening and selecting suitable families, there was an unmistakeable air of urgency. Because of the short Alaskan season for building and farming, any delays in the hastily arranged plans would mean postponing the project for a year, so time was of the essence, and most families had to make almost immediate decisions about whether or not they wanted to be part of the project. If they did, they had precious little time to ready themselves for the life-changing trip, and for some, that meant a matter of only a few days.

The 1935 Matanuska Colony Project

Orlando Miller described the cross-country travels of the first group of families in his book, *The Frontier in Alaska and the Matanuska Colony*:

"Before leaving home, the colonists disposed of inadequate or unsuitable clothing and furniture and were supplied with replacements by the state relief authorities. Those from Minnesota gathered at St. Paul, where they heard a lecture on Alaska by a former member of the faculty of the University of Alaska. They traveled across the country in railroad day coaches, followed and interviewed by newspapermen, and were greeted in San Francisco with speeches and dinners. Before they sailed on May 1, they were given toys for the children, a motion picture projector and film to amuse them during the voyage, and a farewell concert by a hillbilly band. Newspaper accounts described the excited children, tearful women, and grave men, all facing a great adventure, a little frightened but determined."

Chicago Daily Tribune, April 28, 1935 - "270 Minnesotans Depart for New Homes in Alaska."

Chicago Daily Tribune, May 2, 1935 - "274 Board Transport for New Homes in Alaskan Valley."

In October, 1920, fifteen years before it would be pressed into service for the Matanuska Colony, the transport ship *St. Mihiel* was launched for the United States Shipping Board, destined to be operated by the United States Army Transportation Corps. Built by the American International Shipbuilding Corporation in Hog Island, Pennsylvania, the *St. Mihiel* was 448 feet long, weighed 7,500 tons, had a capacity of 800 passengers, a speed of 15.5 knots and a cruising range of 24 days.

Named for the Battle of Saint-Mihiel, France, a World War I battle fought in September, 1918, under the command of General John J. "Black Jack" Pershing, the ship saw frequent travels to Alaskan waters. In the spring of 1935, the *St. Mihiel* was chartered for six months and dispatched to San Francisco to await arrival of the Matanuska Colony families.

The 1935 Matanuska Colony Project

The *North Star* was a Bureau of Indian Affairs ship which, among other duties, delivered supplies for medical and educational services to isolated villages in Alaska. Chartered for service along with the *St. Mihiel* by Colony manager Don Irwin, the *North Star* sailed from San Francisco on April 23, 1935. Aboard were Irwin and many other officials, several assistants, an architect, a photographer, several construction supervisors, and 118 transient workers who would be starting construction of the Colony buildings. Tents, stoves, trucks, tractors, well-drilling equipment and other necessities for creating the new colony were supplemented by massive orders of lumber from Alaska's southeastern forests, brought aboard at Ketchikan and Juneau.

The Christian Science Monitor, April 22, 1935 - "San Francisco: Midwest Exodus to Alaska Valley Is Under Way. The motorship *North Star*, loaded with picked men and farm equipment, ready for first trip to 'promised land' for impoverished farmers on marginal lands of several states. Planned Economy Forty Acres Each. Creaking winches and groaning cargo booms hummed the overture here yesterday to another American epic of adventure and pioneering-- the impending departure of a new band of pilgrims for a promised land."

Ironwood, Michigan is the westernmost city in the state, an iron mining town close to the shores of Lake Superior. In the late spring of 1935 the local newspaper, the *Ironwood Daily Globe,* reported that 67 farm families in neighboring Wisconsin were ready to begin the long trek from their homes to the Matanuska Valley in far-off Alaska.

"Mrs. Winifred Ferguson, field representative of the Wisconsin Emergency Relief Administration, selected the families after a long survey throughout the state. 'They are all very eager and exceptionally enthusiastic over the prospect of carving out new and better homes in Alaska,' she said. 'I painted a not too bright picture of Alaska to many, but virtually all were ready and eager to gamble hard work and hardships against a chance to become independent.'

The 1935 Matanuska Colony Project

"Tomorrow the prospective Alaska settlers will load their choicest belongings on freight trains. They are limited to 2,000 pounds so most are expected to leave behind inexpensive furniture, machinery, etc., and to take musical instruments, and any other articles having a monetary or sentimental value.'"

Spokane Daily Chronicle, April 26, 1935 - "Get a New Chance in Alaska - New hope has come to this Arcadia, Mich. family, a chance to escape from relief rolls and start life over as pioneers in far-off Alaska. Mr. and Mrs. Thomas Synder are among the first of 200 midwest families to be chosen for the United States rural rehabilitation colony in the Matanuska valley and will leave San Francisco in May. Son Billy is all ready and wherever Billy goes, his lamb is sure to go, too."

The Washington Post, May 12, 1935 - "Green Bay, Wis., May 11. 67 Wisconsin Farm Families Off to Alaska. Party Numbering 317 in All. Pioneers New Land in FERA Project. With hopeful visions of the future eclipsing the sadness of hurried farewells, a group of sturdy Wisconsin families today severed bonds of kinship and friendship and started the first lap of a journey to Alaska -- their land of promise."

In the 1930's there was no bridge spanning the five mile wide Straits of Mackinac which connected the upper and lower peninsulas of Michigan. In late April, 1935, the *Ironwood Daily Globe* detailed the impending departure of the settlers' train from St. Ignace, at the southeastern tip of the Upper Peninsula. The specially chartered train had begun the trip in Sault St. Marie, in the far northeastern end of the peninsula, across the border from its twin city of Salt Ste. Marie, Ontario. The train would make its way westward along the Upper Peninsula, making scheduled stops to take aboard groups of families along the route:

"One hundred fifty-nine members of 36 Michigan families will leave here (St. Ignace) at 3 o'clock this afternoon for Alaska. Twenty-nine other Michigan families will entrain at Manistique to make the trip with the

Wisconsin contingent. Two other Michigan families will leave with the group going from Rhinelander.

"Four baggage cars were packed with provisions and personal belongings of pioneers in the train here. Dogs, cats, and one canary were brought to the train and put in a baggage car."

The *Ironwood Daily Globe* continued explaining the complex logistics in an article datelined from Green Bay, Wisconsin, the same day:

"The nine families of about 80 men, women, and children from the northeastern section of the state will entrain tonight at 8:45 o'clock (central standard time) for St. Paul. Meanwhile, another train starting from Sault Ste. Marie with emigrants from Michigan, the third state participating in the project, will be speeding westward to Superior, Wisconsin. Another train will leave with colonists from north central Wisconsin from Rhinelander at 2 a.m. tomorrow. The Sault train will pick up others from northwestern Wisconsin at Superior at 8 a.m., and all trains will meet at St. Paul from where the group will travel on to Seattle."

A staff reporter for the *San Francisco Chronicle*, Carolyn Anspacher, was one of the many writers who wrote glowing reports of the Colonists' trip across the country. Evangeline Atwood wrote about her in *We Shall Be Remembered*; Anspacher joined the families in St. Paul and rode with them to San Francisco, penning these memorable lines along the way:

"The last of the covered wagons is rushing through the night. The great trek from America's main street to Alaska's wilderness is on. Sixty-seven drought-stricken families, 285 men, women, and children are jam-packed into 21 coaches–a modern version of yesterday's ox-drawn wagon. They sit here now, in endless diaper-hung coaches, wearing trappings of a civilization that has swept them to ruin. The same spirit to motivate their fathers and forefathers in seeking out new land is driving them onward. They hope to hew for themselves an economic freedom in a new land.

"The picnic gaiety which crept into the departure from the railroad station, as the brass bands were playing, began to fade as the gas lamps of the old-fashioned cars were lighted and the small children were wrapped in blankets for the night. Then men and women sat silently, their faces chiseled into masks of weariness and frustration. Some complained loudly that the government had promised them Pullman sleepers and here they were having to ride in plain day coaches.

"Of this group, 128 are children, 62 under 12 years of age, 66 under five. There are 21 babes in arms, the youngest being 15 days old. Small grimy faces peer from behind high plush chairs and laugh at life and the splendid excitement of choo-choos.

"In the baggage car where H. L. Richards, in charge of the government project, and his assistants are headquartered, are six dogs that couldn't be left behind. 'We'll need 'em,' said a blond young man crisply. 'We're going to have cattle, and dogs know how to round 'em up better'n men do. As a matter of fact, we need six more collies or shepherds or police dogs, who can stand the climate and who'll work with us.'

Already the colonists, recruited from all parts of the state, have become a closely knit community. During the day, women, until last Friday strangers, are planning how they'll make comfortable homes. A few read, but for the most part they talk quietly, seriously, about a tomorrow that is almost with them.

"Of the group, six are registered nurses who have already been pressed into service by the government physician aboard. Two are college graduates and upper grade teachers.

"For the children, the trip so far has been crowded with excitement. They have eaten enormously in the diners and have been pampered and petted by train officials. They are wearing new clothes provided in most cases by the government and for the moment baths are out of the question.

"Besides, every night in every car just before bedtime, there's a concert. It's not a regulation orchestra, but zithers, mandolins, guitars, mouth organs and accordions do very well.

"Little by little the train quieted down for the night. Upright chairs miraculously became beds. Flowered quilts and striped pillows appeared. A pleasant lassitude came over the colonists–a bride of four days hid her face on the shoulder of her young husband, yawning prodigiously. 'Abide with me,' hummed a sad voice. 'Fast falls the eventide–the darkness deepens. Lord with me abide–when other helpers fail and comforts flee–help of the helpess–O, abide with me.'"

In *We Shall Be Remembered,* Evangeline Atwood described what happened when the train reached California:

"In preparation for their arrival in San Francisco, tall John S. Givens, Jr., government sociologist and rural rehabilitation expert who was to accompany the group to Alaska, entered each car accompanied by officials of the Federal Transient Bureau in San Francisco. Families were tagged, each toddling child properly identified, and baggage carefully marked. The group was divided into three parts, each going to a different hotel and each family supervised by a federal social worker.

"The colonists were told that San Francisco was set to give them a warm and enthusiastic welcome. The children were carefully washed and dressed in their shabby best. Red, blue, and yellow berets found their way out of gaping suitcases. Suits were brushed, shoes polished, babies nursed, and an unnatural calm settled over everyone. The camaraderie and gaiety of the past days disappeared as they realized they were reaching another significant milestone on their long trek to their new home.

"The train pulled into the Southern Pacific Station at Third and Townsend streets, and a SERA band was playing 'Happy Days Are Here Again.' The waiting crowd sent up cheer after cheer as the colonists appeared on the platform, lugging suitcases, bird cages, guitars, and other personal effects.

"Mayor Angelo Rossi, wearing a frock coat, accompanied by Police Chief Quinn and Fire Chief Brennan, stepped forward and began shaking hands, extending the city's official welcome. Hundreds of townspeople crowded forward to wish the colonists good luck."

Atwood shared a few lines from the Mayor's enthusiastic greeting: "I regard these good people making this long, arduous, yet thrilling journey with as great respect as I would were one of the forty-niners to rise from his grave and tell me he had sailed around the Horn to these sunny shores so long ago. They are valiant, every one of them, and I want every moment of their two days' stay in San Francisco to be filled with delight and pleasure."

In Brigitte Lively's book, *The Matanuska Colony, Fifty Years*, Colonist Laurence Vasanoja, writing after their departure aboard the *St. Mihiel*, described the reception they had received in a letter to his brother and sister in Minnesota:

"They sure gave us some welcome signs all over (Welcome Alaska Colonists), the city band, the Mayor and Chief of Police met us at the depot and escorted us to our hotel. They gave us street car tickets, theater tickets, fruit and presents for the kids, and again yesterday on board ship the captain and nurse dished out birthday cake, candy and presents to the kids, and movies were taken of the whole performance. We have several news agents and Paramount Sound Movie operator on board. When we left Frisco there must have been at least eight movie cameras clicking and fifty newspaper cameramen; they shot 3-4 pictures at a time. Must have been some 3500 or 4000 people seeing us off, mostly curiosity seekers and newspapermen. Someday you may see us on the newsreels in moving pictures."

In 1990 a report was written for the U.S. Department of the Interior's National Register of Historic Places, titled *The Settlement and Economic Development of Alaska's Matanuska-Susitna Valley*. Prepared by Fran Seager-Boss, Archeologist; and Lawrence E. Roberts, Historian, the report opened the door to permanent protection for many of the Colony buildings and related structures. Seager-Boss and Roberts deftly explained the fascination factor of the Colony families:

"Seizing on the romance of pioneering, the media provided extensive coverage on the colonists. Newspaper editorials commented that the 'eyes of the world' were upon the colonists. Entertained by big city mayors and interviewed by journalists while traveling from the Lakes states to California for their departure, the colonists became overnight celebrities."

"Part of the colonists' appeal to America was a result of the then strong Agrarian/Frontier myth. Many Americans believed that a simple agrarian existence was more virtuous than other types of labor. And the Great Depression, still going strong, presented a powerful case against free market industrialization. Perhaps Alaska, in spite of Fredrick Jackson Turner's pronouncement that the frontier was closed, could provide a safety valve for the population."

Writing in an unusual third-person format, Colony Manager Don L. Irwin wrote of his unexpectedly complicated trip north in his book, *The Colorful Matanuska Valley*:

"Irwin left Washington April 20 and flew to San Francisco. He took passage on the North Star, Bureau of Indian Affairs boat, along with several people on his staff. Colonel Frank U. Bliss and his staff, in charge of the transient workers, were also on the boat. In addition, 150 transient workers from the California transient camps were being brought to Alaska to help with the land clearing and home construction of the colonists. The North Star was delayed, it stopped at Ketchikan and Juneau to take on lumber, kitchen ranges, and other colony supplies. It arrived in Seward almost at the same time as the *St. Mihiel*, bringing up the Minnesota colonists.

"Irwin was detained in Juneau for three days conferring with the three incorporators of the Alaska Rural Rehabilitation Corporation. The incorporators were hostile at first because they were not being advised by the Washington officials of F.E.R.A. what was being done. Finally, after a particularly heated session, Mr. E. W. Griffin, Territorial Secretary and one of the incorporators, said 'Mr. Irwin, it is our fault that we are not handling the affairs of this project. The incorporating papers came in February during the legislative session. They didn't get out of the Governor's office until after the legislature adjourned in April. I wasn't so busy but what I could have taken care of that matter. We owe you an apology.' Irwin had the full cooperation of the Incorporating Board for the remainder of his stay in Juneau.

"On May 8, Miss Gladys Forrest, Secretary for the Alaska Relief Office, L. N. Troast, Colony architect, and Irwin flew to Fairbanks on the PAA. They came by rail on a gas car from Fairbanks to Matanuska on May 9. Next day they were at Palmer on the location of camp site No. 1 helping prepare for the arrival of the Minnesota colonists' families."

As the Colonists, project officials, and other contingents gathered and made their way north, there were rumblings from pioneer Alaskans who voiced misgivings about the whole idea. The Alaska Territorial Chamber of Commerce actually passed a resolution stating that if the Colony failed the state would be saddled with hundreds of indigents needing food, clothing, and shelter. The territorial legislature insisted that Secretary of the Interior Harold Ickes and Alaska Delegate Anthony Dimond take steps to provide adequate funds for the potential failure of the project–including return passage to the west coast for the would-be settlers.

The *Anchorage Times* weighed in on the side of the Colonists, saying the project might prove to be the most economically constructive idea for the territory to ever come out of Washington. Publisher Robert Atwood was a strong supporter of the Colony Project, and the *Anchorage Times* chided the nay-sayers by pointing out that Alaska had been exploited many times over the years by absentee interests, but the Colonists were cut from a different cloth and they were coming to Alaska to build homes and help settle the land.

When the legislature balked at appropriating funds to build schools for the Colonists' children, the *Anchorage Times* took them to task, asking: "Is the territory going to establish a precedent against expanding its school services to additional population? Where would other states be if they called a halt on schools after they received their first pioneer settlers?"

The legislature subsequently approved the expenditure of $100,000 for additional school facilities in the Matanuska Valley.

Ironwood Daily Globe, Ironwood, Michigan. May 15, 1935 - "Mr. and Mrs. Walter Anderson and families left Monday night by special train for

St. Paul, Minn., where they joined others on the trip to the Matanuska Valley in Alaska. Mr. and Mrs. Anderson have five children, the youngest being six months old.

"On Friday evening the community gave a farewell party at the town hall for the Anderson family. Music was furnished by Camp 662 orchestra. Dancing and games were enjoyed. At 11:30 lunch was served to a large number of friends. Supt. H.O. Johnson gave a farewell speech. A purse of money was given to Mr. and Mrs. Anderson from the community."

Bakersfield Californian, May 15, 1935 - Green Bay, Wisc., May 14. "400 Persons on Their Way from Wisconsin and Michigan to Alaskan Valley. Spirits high as they envisioned the thrills of starting life over again in a strange land, more than 400 pioneers from Wisconsin and upper Michigan today were rolling westward in a steam-driven Mayflower toward new homes in Alaska. While crated dogs barked and whined in coaches up front and children of all ages roamed from seat to seat through the long train, the adults chosen by the federal government to colonize the Matanuska Valley under a FERA project were acquainting themselves with new neighbors. Nine families from northeastern Wisconsin and six from Minominee County, Mich., 103 persons in all, left here last night. The remainder of the 67 Wisconsin families entrained at Rhinelander and Superior, and those from Michigan at Sault Ste. Marie. Tears were shed, but mostly by kinfolk gathered for farewell on the site of old Fort Howard. Their noses flattened against windows, the children received adieus from those on the platforms while parents waved happy responses.

"'It's a chance that comes once in a lifetime,' said Kenneth Foster, of Menominee County, Michigan, as he sat in the coach with his wife, Marlon, and one boy. Some were from farms, others from small towns, but all were vigorous, sturdy, and high spirited with the prospect of earning a livelihood of which they had been deprived in the states. Leaving st. Paul with the remainder of the Wisconsin and Michigan group, the colonists will embark from Seattle Saturday on board the U.S.S. *St. Mihiel* for the six-day trip on the Pacific to Seward."

The 1935 Matanuska Colony Project

Ironwood Daily Globe, Ironwood, Michigan. May 15, 1935 - "Biggest Brood Among the Alaskan Pioneers." The new 'pioneer colony' in Alaska's Matanuska Valley is going to thrive, prosper, and grow if the family of Williams Bouwens of Rhinelander, Wis. is any criterion. The Bouwens, in taking all their 11 children with them, make up the largest complete family among the emigrants. Bouwens is a skilled butcher, and a deputy sheriff."

In Brigette Lively's book, *Matanuska Colony Fifty Years*, the daughter of Colonists Irving and Lila Newville, Dorothy Woods, described what it was like to set off from Seattle, voicing a feeling and an experience which was undoubtedly shared by many of the colonists:

"Boarding the boat was exciting. A lot of us had never seen an ocean, even the boat was something I had not seen. It was all very wonderful until we started to pull away from the pier with the band playing and most of Seattle at the dock seeing us off. Then came the thoughts of how final this adventure was. My Mom tells of her misgivings, there were tears and second thoughts."

The trip to Alaska was formally underway and there was no recourse now. Six mothers remained in Seattle with their children because of illness, while their husbands traveled ahead with the other Colonists on the *St. Mihiel* to be present for the drawing of land tracts. The women and children would later make the trip to Alaska on the *North Star*.

One of the most compelling and detailed publications on the 1935 Matanuska Colony Project is a study undertaken for the government's Interior-Agriculture Committee on Group Settlement in Alaska, which was intended as a factual, objective appraisal of the project.

The report, *Alaskan Group Settlement: The Matanuska Valley Colony*, by Kirk H. Stone of the University of Wisconsin, was published in 1950 by the United States Department of the Interior. A 95-page side-stapled booklet, the publication offers valuable insights to the project, such as this commentary on the transportation expenses:

"Moving the colonists possibly cost about $70,000. Exact figures cannot be obtained. It is known that $18,436 was paid by the colonists' home states for transportation to the west coast. The Corporation's expense for chartering the *St. Mihiel* was $60,000 and for the *North Star* was approximately $10,000; however, each ship was used to haul equipment and supplies as well as colonists and possibly half of the expenses are chargeable to general organization of The Colony. What the ARRC paid the Alaska Railroad is not obtainable but it is estimated that shipment of the colonists and their effects cost about $12,000. Originally these costs of transportation were to be paid by Michigan, Minnesota, and Wisconsin with funds from the F.E.R.A. However, the records indicate that the Corporation assumed all of the expenses of the colonists after they reached the west coast. Although the funds for colonization eventually came from the same source, the Corporation's assumption cost probably $50,000 that were not budgeted in the plans for The Colony."

"They are America's new pioneers and perhaps the first of the last." ~Arville Schaleben

Chapter Eight

To Build A Community

As the Colonists were making their way north to Alaska, officials and workers were scrambling to make certain there were at least the beginnings of a community to meet them upon their arrival. Don Irwin shared a letter in his book, *The Colorful Matanuska Valley*, which described the situation in Palmer preceding the arrival of the first families:

Alaska Rural Rehabilitation Corporation - Juneau

Matanuska Colonization Project
Palmer, Alaska

June 11, 1935

MEMORANDUM
TO: D. L. Irwin, General Manager
FROM: Francis L. Biggs, Asst. Super. Architect
Re: Construction period, May 6 to 16

On arrival at Palmer, Alaska, about 3:00 p.m. on May 6, 1935, in conjunction with Ross L. Sheely, decided on the location of the colonists' main camp site and immediately proceeded with the layout of 69 tents to

Cabin construction with the numbered logs. Note 2x8's cut at the mill being used for floor construction. ASL-P270-479 by Willis T. Geisman. ARRC Album, Mary Nan Gamble Collection, Alaska State Library.

accommodate the first contingent of colonists due to arrive Friday afternoon, May 10, 1935.

Eleven carpenters and laborers engaged locally as the only available labor, the transients being occupied with the erection of their own camp, immediately proceeded to erect tent frames and haul lumber from the railroad siding to the site of construction activities.

On Wednesday, May 8, 1935, work started at 4:00 a.m. and continued on into the evening and at the end of the day, 13 tents had been erected. On Thursday, May 9, 1935, 85 transient workers, in addition to the eleven carpenters were engaged in filling holes for outhouses. Work started at 4:00 a.m. and continued on into the evening with a total of 28 tents completed and frames and floors erected for approximately 30 others.

On Friday, May 10, 1935, work started at 4:00 a.m. and about 5:00 p.m. 69 tents were ready near the railroad siding for families and 4 outhouses completed. This included the installation of kitchen ranges and single bed mattresses. All this was about 15 minutes before the arrival of the train bringing the Minnesota colonists to Palmer.

On Friday a commissary was erected, and on Saturday, the 11th, a warehouse was started and completed about the 16th of May.

During the construction period between the 7th and 16th, 70 tents were completed and 6 double outhouses, also commissary and warehouse.

Signed Francis L. Biggs
Asst. Supervising Architect
and Director of Construction

The transients mentioned in Biggs' memorandum to Don Irwin were a key factor in the Colony Project. The Civilian Conservation Corps, popularly known as the CCC, was a New Deal public work relief program which operated from 1933 to 1942 for unemployed, unmarried men between the ages of 18 to 28. In exchange for a day's labor, the program provided them with shelter, clothing, and food, together with a small wage of $30 a month, $25 of which had to be sent home to their families. During the short span of years when the CCC was active, workers planted nearly 3 billion trees to help reforest America, constructed more than 800 parks nationwide, upgraded most state parks, and built a network of service buildings and public roadways in remote areas, including many parks projects and public buildings in Alaska. The most popular of all the New Deal programs, Congress voted to end the CCC in 1942, when the draft was initiated for World War II. CCC alumni would later include test pilot Chuck Yeager, baseball player Stan Musial, environmentalist Aldo Leopold, and actors Walter Matthau, Raymond Burr, and Robert Mitchum.

In the spring of 1935 approximately 400 of these CCC men were selected from the state of California and given the task of doing the early clearing and building for the Colony. On April 23, 118 of the transient men sailed north from San Francisco aboard the *North Star*, along with the project officials and most of the materials and building supplies. The remaining 280 workers sailed on the *St. Mihiel* with the colonists, arriving in the seaport town of Seward, Alaska, at almost the same time. Evangeline Atwood noted that the transient workers were the first to step off the ship as they would be traveling through the night to Anchorage, en route to Palmer to get ready the tent camp. She colorfully described the arrival of the transient men in Anchorage:

"With the arrival of six hundred transient workers about noon the following day, Anchorage knew its next-door neighbors had really arrived. Like the advance guard of an invading army, the workers poured off the train, throwing baggage and bedding onto the little depot platform with such abandon that the onlookers had to run for cover to avoid being hit by bedrolls as they sailed through the air. The men were rigged out in heavy leather boots, raincoats, leather coats, slickers, and rubber shoepacks. They even had hats covered with black mosquito netting, and cans of Buhac stuck out from their emergency kits. Most of them were young, husky, and raring to start their northland adventure. They stopped just long enough to grab a sandwich and a cup of coffee before going on to Palmer.

"Frank U. Bliss, of Santa Barbara, was in charge of the party. He was to serve as director of construction for the project. Colonel Ohlson was surrounded by a bevy of newsmen and newsreel cameramen. The spotlight of the nation's press was angled squarely on this daring and somewhat dubious undertaking. Some of the writers and photographers were to remain with the colonists for several weeks."

Colonel Otto F. Ohlson, noted in the article, had been general manager of the Alaska Railroad since 1928, and he was also chairman of the Alaska Rural Rehabilitation Corporation, as well as one of the founding leaders of the Matanuska Colony Project. Described as an energetic, quick-tempered man, Ohlson had been referred to as "Colonel" since World War I, when he directed military railroad operations in France. After more than 20 years working with the Pennsylvania and Northern Pacific Railroads, he recommended a colonization program for the debt-ridden Alaska Railroad which had slowly, inexorably, evolved into the Matanuska Colony Project.

A United Press article in *The Daily Times*, published in Rochester, Pennsylvania, dated May 29, 1935, detailed the work of the transients in laying the groundwork for the Matanuska Colony Project:

"Transients in Alaska Colony. Five hundred recruited from the transient camps of California form the backbone of the federal colonization of the Matanuska Valley of Alaska.

"Homeless themselves, they are building the homes in which 200 families from the midwest will be housed before November in a valley rimmed by snowclad peaks and lighted by a sun which shines almost 24 hours a day at the beginning of summer and not at all in the winter.

"The construction corps is a group apart. The colonists avoid contact with the men. Alaska's Chamber of Commerce protested their coming, fear their continued presence. Misunderstood and maligned, they are held together by a single desire–the desire to work.

"It hurt the men's pride a lot when Alaskans protested they were 'riff-raff' and feared that when the Matanuska job is finished the transients would remain in Alaska to glut an already overcrowded market for common labor.

"Federal authorities took one precaution to insure their departure from Alaska when the job is done. None of them will be paid off until they reach Seattle. In the meantime they will be given $2 a week spending money, and they'll have difficulty spending that in a valley where there are no entertainment facilities and where the only business enterprise is a general store which handles only foodstuffs, candy, and tobacco.

"The Construction Corps is quartered in a tent city two miles from the colonists' camp. They have their own mess and their own work duties. Theirs is the heavy work on the project–the building of the townsite with its community buildings, the fashioning of the logs from which the cabins will be built, construction of highways to replace the muddy roads now winding aimlessly through the valley."

Herbert Henry Hilscher came to Alaska with his parents in 1906, at the age of four. A lifelong writer and newspaperman, a delegate to the Alaska Constitutional Convention, an avid historian, and a founder and first president of the Cook Inlet Historical Society, he wrote four books about Alaska, including the wide-ranging *Alaska Now* published by Little, Brown & Company in 1948. In that book, in a chapter titled "Matanuska in One Easy Lesson," Hilscher wrote:

"The most important event in the well-publicized life of the Matanuska Valley was not the circus parade of 890 persons from the states of Minnesota, Wisconsin and Michigan to Alaska in 1935 as guests of the United States Treasury Department."

The 'most important event,' according to Hilscher, was the arrival of a six-pound package of seed potatoes at the Matanuska Experimental Farm in December of 1932. A farmer at Wiseman, a small mining community in the Brooks Range, along the Middle Fork of the Koyukuk River and above the Arctic Circle, had developed the hardy variety. He sent a box to the Station near Palmer, and by the time Hilscher wrote his book the descendants of those nine superior potatoes comprised "fully three quarters of all the potatoes grown in the Matanuska-Anchorage area."

Hilscher continued:

"These potatoes were lifted from obscurity and developed into a standard potato variety by a raw-boned, six-foot Irishman named Don

Irwin. Don inherited the Arctic unknowns along with the managership of the Matanuska Experiment Station in the middle of 1934.

"Irwin brought to Alaska an intimate knowledge of big-scale Kansas farming and 18 years' experience in ranching and potato growing in Wyoming. He had a 'potato-eye,' and on his first tour around the experimental farm spotted the unnamed Wiseman potatoes. In comparison with other potatoes in the experimental field they were bigger, the vines stronger, the leaves broader."

Hilscher described how Don Irwin championed what he named the Arctic Seedling potato, and then explained:

"Don Irwin's work with Alaskan potatoes was interrupted for a time when he was called back to Washington and drafted to be the first manager of the Matanuska Colony. This quiet, blue-eyed agronomist, who has the ability to work well with people, submitted his recommendations, built on years of farming experience, had them accepted, and returned to Alaska to carry them out."

The *Anchorage Daily Times* publisher's wife, Evangeline Atwood, underscored Irwin's key role in the Colony Project in her 1966 book, *We Shall Be Remembered*:

"An early decision was to make Irwin the resident general manager of the project in Alaska. Had the same degree of wisdom been used in other planning areas, many unnecessary mistakes could have been avoided. In addition to a long record of experience and training in agricultural affairs, Irwin had personal attributes that made him uniquely fitted for the job. He had a genial disposition, a broad tolerance, infinite patience and understanding in human relationships, an ever-present sense of humor, and a large capacity for hard work.

"It was the solid figure of Don Irwin, working quietly and unobtrusively in the background during those first hectic months, that held the colony together. He had the knack of making the lonely, the frustrated, the disillusioned colonists feel that he cared about their troubles and that he stood ready to help them overcome their difficulties and disappointments."

The 1935 Matanuska Colony Project

An article in the *Bend Bulletin*, published in Bend, Oregon, May 9, 1935, headlined "Canvas Towns Rise in North," told the story of the beginnings of the Colony and the impending arrival of the new settlers:

"White tents sprawled over the green Matanuska river valley today, reflecting the bright hope of 67 midwestern farm families driven from their homes by drouth and dust and seeking a new life in Alaska.

"Two hundred of the structures, aligned in neat rows by 500 CCC workers, made up one city of temporary dwellings, where the American colonists will live until their experimental farming venture gets underway in earnest.

"Two miles distant, another canvas town was constructed as quarters for the workers themselves, advance guard for the migration to come.

"The first contingent of settlers, 67 families from the dust and drouth denuded farming areas of Minnesota, are at Seward, awaiting completion of preliminary work here. They will live in the tent city until the remaining families of colonizers arrive from Seattle later this month.

"When the full contingent has arrived, government supervisors for the project will stage a drawing in which the most desirable tracks will be allotted over the 8000 acre tract set aside for the farming colony.

"Each family will receive 40 acres of land, on which modern homes, capable of withstanding an Alaskan winter, will be constructed by fall.

"While their elders strolled about Seward, children of the party remained in quarantine aboard the U. S. Army transport *St. Mihiel*. The quarantine was imposed as a precautionary measure when five children of the party were stricken with measles.

"Old residents of the region are skeptical of success of the new venture. Damp soil, they believe, will not produce fine vegetables and markets are slight for such produce. Work in the field will be hampered by large mosquitos. Farmers of the region must wear mosquito netting suspended from headgear to escape the insects' attacks.

"But, if at the end of five years the colony is flourishing, others probably will be established in other more temperate sections of Alaska, advancing the territory another step toward statehood."

The 1935 Matanuska Colony Project

Kirk H. Stone's landmark 1950 report, *Alaskan Group Settlement: The Matanuska Valley Colony*, prepared for the U. S. Department of the Interior, Bureau of Land Management, explained the arrangements made for official business and social purposes in the early months:

"The Colony had no facilities for community services in the beginning. Palmer was only a branch railroad siding. To supply the facilities, architects drafted a model plan for a Community Center. The plan, approved a year after colonization began, included buildings for the servicing of a cooperative agricultural community.

"The Community Center was built at Palmer siding. The site selected was the flat land just to the east of the railroad tracks and station. The original plan called for the establishment of a village at a road junction in the center of The Colony where all of the colonists would live and from which the people would migrate daily to their farms. Four Corners, about four and a half miles west of Palmer, was the logical point for such a village but the needed land could not be bought. Matanuska Junction was also suggested as a center. But Mr. Irwin anticipated flooding of that site; indeed, it was under water in the first year of colonization and flooding since then has been a major reason why settlers have abandoned Matanuska Junction.

"Critics of the site at Palmer siding have stated that the Community Center should have been built on the rough land less than half a mile west of the present site or on that land a mile or two southwestward and on the railroad. Such criticism is unsound. Accessibility is fundamental in Alaska and the Palmer site is beside the railroad and close to the point where the Matanuska River is most easily and cheaply bridged by the Palmer Highway which, also, makes accessible all the land in the Butte District. Too, the Community Center required less than 40 acres of better farming land and the whole village of Palmer covered fewer than 250 acres in 1948.

"However, a better location than the one adopted would have been the junction of the railroad and the Palmer Highway, one-half mile northward from the present site. The junction was considered but the homesteaders who owned the adjoining land in 1935 would not sell it. Since 1935 the land has been sold and Palmer has grown toward the junction, resulting in a less compact pattern of buildings in the village than might otherwise have developed.

"Temporary facilities were used for community services in the first year of colonization. School classes were held in railroad cars and colonists' homes. Administration was from tent-offices. Church services were held in homes and in a small building put up by the colonists in 1935. (It is perhaps embarrassing to the clergy to be reminded that materials for the church seemed to appear out of thin air!) At Palmer, also, a hastily erected warehouse and a trading center served as points from which the colonists were supplied equipment and obtained food and clothing. There was no marketing problem in the first year because practically no land was cleared for cropping and little farming was done. Administrative personnel were supplied temporary housing in the form of tents and partially completed staff houses and dormitory. Hospitalization was in the church building after it was quickly converted because of an epidemic and the staff was composed of one doctor and a few nurses. Stoves and lanterns supplied heat and light. Recreation was largely a matter for individual action–there was too much confusion and everyone was too busy. It was impossible for a whole community to be built at once on so large a scale as was tried. However, permanent facilities for community services were well established at the Center by the end of 1936."

The Milwaukee Journal, May 6, 1935. "Alaska Ready - Except Valley. Matanuska area work slowed up so pioneers face delay. Seward, Alaska (AP) Everything was ready Monday for the government's Matanuska colonists–except the Matanuska Valley.

"The 67 Minnesota farm families are scheduled to arrive here on the Army transport *St. Mihiel* Monday evening. They will find bands playing, flags waving, harbor craft whistles screaming and the entire population of this picturesque town turned out to greet them.

"And the first thing they'll view will be 'depression's end.' Seward had a labor shortage on its docks. Nine winchmen's jobs alone went begging for men Saturday, all because eight gold finds in recent weeks have drawn most of the jobless out prospecting.

"Plans to speed the colonists to the valley were disrupted, however, because the *St. Mihiel* is arriving so closely on the heels of the North Star, which docked here only Saturday night. The latter brought a contingent of transient workers who were dispatched to the valley to start building shelter for the families.

"The colonists must wait here for several days until the tent homes and other necessary structures are erected. Not only is there a lack of housing in the Matanuska valley, but reports at Anchorage were that surveying of farms for allotment to the colonists was not completed. The weather in the Matanuska, however, is mild. The snow is all gone and resident farmers of the district are preparing their fields for spring work.

"Colony managers are confident the movement will swing along splendidly after a few days. All available cars were sent here from Anchorage to speed the transients and their lumber and other supplies over the Alaska Railroad to Palmer, selected as the community center for the new pioneers.

"Aboard *St. Mihiel*–Alaska Bound. (AP) Sixty-seven migrating farm families aboard this transport learned Monday that their trip to the Matanuska valley will be delayed three days at Seward. All the families will continue to live on the transport until they are moved inland.

"As the *St. Mihiel* steamed through the Pacific off the coast of Alaska the weather became colder but there was no illness on the ship and all the colonists appeared cheerful and eager for the work ahead."

Berkeley Gazette, Berkeley, California. May 4, 1935. "Farm Families Reach Alaska for New Battle with Nature." James Sullivan, United Press Staff Correspondent. "Seward, Alaska, May 7. Defeated once by the ravages of dust and drought, 67 farm families from midwestern United States today awaited start of their second conflict with nature. They arrived here last night after six impatient days at sea aboard the U. S. Army transport *St. Mihiel*. Their arrival marked completion of the second step of their great adventure which will determine whether they will wrest a living from the fertile soil of Matanuska Valley or will succumb a second time to the unpredictable caprices of the elements. Indications were that they will not begin the last leg of the journey to their new homes at Palmer, in Matanuska Valley, for several days."

Anchorage welcomed the Matanuska Colony families with open arms on May 10, 1935, in a city-wide celebration which had been planned for weeks ahead of time. Mayor Oscar Gill and Chamber of Commerce President Winfield Ervin, Sr., shook hands with everyone as they descended from the train, and news reporters and cameramen delighted in capturing the landmark event. Then the families were loaded into cars for the trip to the Anchorage community hall for a true Alaskan feast. Weeks in the planning by the women of Anchorage, the tables groaned with specialties of the Colonists' new home: Moose, salmon, caribou, and buffalo; bountiful vegetable dishes of many varieties; and sauces, jellies, and preserves from native berries of every description. A high school orchestra accompanied the meal, and afterwards there were welcoming speeches, tours along the streets of their new neighbor-to-be, articles in the newspaper, and a warm send-off to their new home in the Valley.

The plans of the many men and women who saw potential in settling the Last Frontier were finally coming to fruition. From the far-sighted visionaries to the hard-working realists, from the pencil-pushing planners to the transient men with their sleeves rolled, the Colony Project was steadily moving closer to becoming a reality. For the colonist families, the long days and nights of traveling by train and ship and wondering what laid ahead were behind them now, and arriving in the Matanuska Valley was a red letter day, marked by green grass and warm sunshine, more handshakes and welcoming speeches, more reporters and newsreel cameramen–and a sobering realization that their greatest adventure was still ahead of them.

Pulling up logs for gable construction. ASL-P270-484 by Willis T. Geisman. ARRC Album, Mary Nan Gamble Collection, Alaska State Library.

"I never dreamed it was as nice as what we saw when we got here." ~Ray Rebarchek

Chapter Nine

New Beginnings

Arville Schaleben was a cub reporter working for *The Milwaukee Journal* in Milwaukee, Wisconsin, when he was presented with the opportunity of a lifetime. The newspaper offered to send the young journalist to Alaska with the Matanuska colonists in return for a series of articles about the government's unusual New Deal experiment.

Schaleben leapt at the offer and travelled to Alaska with the Wisconsin families, living alongside them in the Palmer tent city that first summer, writing and filing stories almost daily - over 150 stories and more than 400 photographs - which appeared in *The Milwaukee Journal* and were also syndicated in newspapers around the country. The resulting series of articles was nominated for a Pulitzer Prize and cemented Schaleben's reputation as a journalist.

Schaleben went on to enjoy a long career at *The Milwaukee Journal*, including serving as managing editor and vice-president at the time of his retirement. He returned to the Matanuska Valley periodically, following up on the remarkable story that he claimed was the best of his long and distinguished career. Schaleben authored a book, *Your Future in Journalism* (Richards Rosen Press, 1961), and his special interests included journalism education and the newspaper's role in a democracy, to which he wrote, "Think a good thought for the man who went out with a paper and pencil and reported facts to you. As long as he is free to ask questions, you are free. As long as his eyes are open, so are yours."

Arville Schaleben shared detailed accounts of the trip across the United States with the Wisconsin and Michigan families, their journey north on the *St. Mihiel*, and the receptions accorded the colonists in Seward, Anchorage, and their new home in the Matanuska Valley. He described their day-to-day hardships and rewards, and brought the Matanuska Colony Project to life for his readers, who could only wonder what it would be like to embark on such an adventure. Eighty years later Arville Schaleben's writing would still be hailed as a monumental effort.

In *The Colorful Matanuska Valley*, Colony Project General Manager Don Irwin shared a description of the first few days of the Matanuska Colony Project:

"When the Minnesota colonists arrived on the evening of May 10, their tents, stoves, and beds were ready. They were fed that evening and the next morning at the transients' mess, which was in some converted Alaska Railroad passenger cars set out on the Palmer siding. All of their bedding and personal effects were in boxes on gondola cars on the railroad siding. One thousand single beds and mattresses were a gift to the project from the California Relief Organization. Bedding was borrowed for the first night from the transient camp, which was being constructed about one mile south of Palmer.

"The Minnesota men were divided into two groups. Trucks were brought up from the transient camp. One group of colonist men worked during the night unloading the boxes of the colonist belongings and placing them in front of the tent which had been numbered and assigned to an individual family. Next day, the other half of the Minnesota men completed the job of unloading personal effects. That day, bedding borrowed from the transients was gathered up from the colonists and returned. Very few of the administrative people working on the project slept during that 48-hour period.

"Since there would be a few days before the arrival of the Wisconsin and Michigan colonist families on May 24, the time was used in getting the other eight camp sites ready for their occupancy. There was machinery to assemble, equipment, supplies, and provisions to be unloaded and stored."

The evening of the colonists' arrival was pleasant enough, but the bucolic weather soon gave way to normal springtime Alaskan weather. "Rain, rain, and more rain," as Irwin described it, made the valley's small network of roads all but impassable, even though the Alaska Road Commission kept their crews working 24 hours per day. Streets and walkways became muddy messes, and the Minnesota housewives struggled to keep their tents neat and clean and their young children somewhat presentable.

A group of colonists gathered to select candidates for their new town's offices, and, realizing that the community needed a name, they selected the descriptively apt 'Valley City,' and erected a large sign on the newspapermens' tent declaring 'Welcome to Valley City.' Colonel Ohlson thought the new town deserved a name with more historical significance, and he chose the name 'Palmer' in honor of the first white man to settle in the Matanuska Valley, George W. Palmer.

Palmer had come to Alaska in 1893 to seek his fortune, and he found it when he struck gold in the mountains of the Kenai Peninsula. A shrewd businessman, he invested in enough goods to stock a small store near the narrow rock-lined canyon of the Matanuska River just east of where the Matanuska colonists would later settle. Widely recognized as one of the first entrepreneurs in that part of Alaska, George Palmer lived among the Dena'ina and by 1900 he was the agent for a small trading post of the Alaska Commercial Company in the then-bustling community of Knik.

A fearless boatman, George Palmer frequently crossed the wide and treacherous Knik Arm between Knik and the Tyonek on the western shore, and the towns of Sunrise, Hope, and Seldovia on the Kenai Peninsula side. Matanuska Valley historian Colleen Mielke wrote: "Palmer's first schooner, the two masted 'C. T. Hill,' arrived at Knik Harbor June 7, 1913. Leaving his store in the hands of a clerk, Palmer and crew sailed the schooner from Goose Bay to San Francisco two or three times a summer and brought back merchandise for his store."

Two years later Palmer traveled to Seward by dogteam, took a steamship down the Inside Passage to San Franciso, purchased a newer schooner named 'The Lucy,' and sailed it home to Knik, arriving on May 3, 1915."

The name 'Palmer,' evoking images of a colorful and ruggedly independent pioneer, would be a fine name for the new frontier town.

The Atlanta Constitution, Atlanta, Georgia, May 13, 1935 - "Travel Weary Pioneers Settle Down As CCC Boys Build Their Homes. Matanuska Valley, Alaska, May 12. Weary after their long journey by land and sea from Minnesota, but well content, the first of the Alaska colonists are setting down happily in their new and strange surroundings."

Historic photographs show parallel rows of neat white cabin-style tents, and inside each tent was a new coal- and wood-burning cookstove, already burning to warm the tent inside and with a bucket of coal alongside for stoking throughout the night. Simple beds with springs, mattresses, sheets, and blankets awaited the tired colonists, and each tent was stocked with food and the basic necessities. Evangeline Atwood colorfully described the scene in the new community after the colonists had enjoyed their first night's sleep in their new tent-homes:

"Smoke curled from the chimneys of a hundred tents the next morning as the Minnesotans unpacked their belongings and one by one stepped outdoors to survey their new home. After a breakfast of grapefruit, cereal, scrambled eggs bread, jelly, and coffee, faces beamed as they looked up at the snow-capped Talkeetna Mountain Range. The sun came out warm and bright. Some of the newcomers discarded the heavy coats with which they had prepared themselves for the Alaska they believed they were entering–a land of ice and snow and cold.

The 1935 Matanuska Colony Project

"All nature smiled as the new citizens began transplanting family roots, which for some of them had been imbedded in Midwestern soil for a century. Much of the countryside reminded them of their own native Minnesota. There were the same kinds of lakes–sparkling bodies of ice-cold water. The trees were almost the same–white-barked birch and evergreens. The soil they found richer and deeper than their own. It was a sandy loam, the choicest patches available in the valley."

The realities of the situation were made clear in the 1990 report for the U.S. Department of the Interior's National Register of Historic Places, titled *The Settlement and Economic Development of Alaska's Matanuska-Susitna Valley*. In an opening section titled Statement of Historic Context, writers Fran Seager-Boss, Archeologist; and Lawrence E. Roberts, Historian, detailed many important aspects of the new community:

"Homesites were concentrated near the community center, which would provde the essential administrative, economic, and social services that would be needed by the new agricultural settlement. The colony would need storage, processing, and marketing facilities; stores, school, community hall, staff offices and housing, cannery, creamery, and other related facilities. FERA's philosophy, as expressed by [FERA architect] Williams, envisioned a 'well-rounded community,' self-sufficient agriculturally, with small allied industries and processing plants.' The entire project would be governed by a 'Settlement Agreement' which specified the responsibilities of both the settlers and the government.

"Each selected colony family was given a charge account and allowed to charge pre-departure expenses for furniture, tools, and household equipment. The Alaska Rural Rehabilitation Corporation (ARRC) was incorporated on April 12, 1935 as a nonprofit entity created by the Rural Rehabilitation Division of FERA to administer the project in Alaska. ARRC agreed to pay the transportation costs of the colonists to the colony, and up to 2,000 pounds of freight per family. Colonists would be housed in tents until their homes were completed. Each family would be able to buy a homestead of at least forty acres, ranging in price from $5.00 per acre for unimproved land to an unspecified amount for cleared or already developed acreage. Payment to the Corporation would be over a thirty year mortgage at three percent interest, with interest to begin accumulating in 1938 and payments to start in 1940.

"The Corporation would provide machinery, livestock, and equipment via sale, lease, rent, or a per use charge. Until they were self sufficient, colonists would get subsistence items at cost, charged to their accounts that they would repay. It was estimated that these expenses would amount to about $3,500 per family by the time they achieved self-reliance (a figure that proved to be much too low). In addition, the ARRC would provide educational, recreational, and health services; supervision of the colony, and consultation to the colonists. Colonists were required to agree to abide by all Corporation rules in conjunction with crop production, processing and marketing, distribution and other measures for the welfare of the community. This emphasis on communal cooperation prompted some critics of New Deal programs to accuse the administration of Socialism and of designing a Communistic community on the order of the Soviet Union's state farms."

Original plans for the colony had called for all of the families to remain in the central tent city while their homes were being constructed, but that plan changed, as noted in a news item in the Spokane, Washington newspaper, the *Spokesman-Review*, dated May 16, 1935: "Matanuska Colonists To Split Into Eight Groups. Palmer, Alaska. May 15. (AP)– The tent city for the Matanuska valley agricultural colonists will be split up into eight different camps upon the arrival here of the colonists from Wisconsin and Michigan, Don Irwin, director of the project, said today.

"One camp, of about 25 tents, will be left here, but the plans to house all the families here have been changed to enable each household to be near their own farms, while the land is being cleared and permanent log houses are under construction, he said."

The second contingent of colonists were traveling to Alaska on the St. Mihiel, the same ship which had earlier brought the Minnesota families.

When the ship docked at Seward on May 22, it was announced that the men were to continue on to Palmer aboard a special train so they would be present for the land tracts drawing which was scheduled for the next day. A hue and cry arose from the women and children at being left behind, but to no avail. They followed by train, arriving in Palmer the next day.

Berkeley Daily Gazette, Berkeley, California, May 24, 1935. "Lands Drawn By Colonists. By United Press. Palmer, Alaska. May 24. Old neighbors in Wisconsin, Michigan, and Minnesota will have adjoining 40-acre tracts in their new land of promise in the Matanuska Valley, following a draw for land today that had the colonists teeming with excitement.

"On a hurriedly constructed rostrum the men filed by Don L. Irwin, manager of the colony, and drew slips of paper from a box that designated their future homes.

"Sighs went up from the women and children who looked on anxiously, as they feared they would be separated by several miles from old friends.

"But the government was not long in restoring their peace of mind with announcement that they might 'swap' slips with other colonists and thus live near their former neighbors of the drought and dust areas of the Mid-West.

"Irwin termed the draw the 'start of a new epoch,' and the colonists agreed with him when he added 'We'll make out all right here.'"

Don Irwin shared details of the land drawing in his 1968 book, *The Colorful Matanuska Valley*:

"On May 23 drawing for home tracts was held. First the men drew from a box held by Ross Sheely, numbers 1 to 202 inclusive. This was the order in which they would stand in line to draw their home tracts.

"The men lined up the second time in numerical order and each drew from a box held by Colonel Ohlson, a small roll of paper fastened by a rubber band. This paper had typed on it a tract number and a legal description of the land drawn. On the evening before the tract drawing the survey crews checked the legal descriptions of each tract for accuracy. Donald McDonald, Sr., father of the Alaska Highway idea, was there to help the engineers check the descriptions. Some tracts contained as much as 80 acres. The majority were 40 acres in area. These numbers and legal descriptions had been entered in a book by Miss Gladys Forrest, Secretary of the Alaska Emergency Relief Office and representative of the ARRC Incorporating Board. She took the name of the colonist who had drawn the tract and entered it alongside the tract number and legal description. Thus were the homesites drawn."

The Milwaukee Journal reporter, Arville Schaleben, gave the most interesting account of the drawing in an article which appeared the next day, May 24. After depicting the gathered colonists, the drawing procedure, and describing how "fate ruled those moments," he wrote:

"The drawing continued for three hours. Some got what they had hoped for, smiled ear to ear, and clapped comrades on the back. Others were disappointed because they would be separated from close friends, or because they would be far from good fishing. All this led to considerable consequent bartering. The men got together and exchanged slips. Some of those who had drawn better tracts demanded something to boot in the exchange–and got it. Others tried to drive too hard a bargain and found no takers. A surprising number were completely satisfied when the drawing and bartering was all over and most of the little groups who had come from Michigan or Wisconsin or Minnesota together had managed to get farms near each other.

"One settler had swapped a strip along the crystal clear Finger Lake to a fishing enthusiast for a tract near town with buildings and 30 acres cleared. That partly cleared farm was considered a particular prize, as indeed it should be, for most of the tracts are covered with brush and light timber."

With their tract locations determined the colonists were moved into the tent camps closest to their new farms, some close in to Palmer and others several miles away, including some closer to the railroad town of Wasilla and a large group across the Matanuska River at Bodenburg Butte. Irwin wrote that the scattered camps "presented two problems. One, for the colonists and the other, for the corporation. Scattered over four townships, as these camps were, some were as much as eight miles from the Palmer headquarters, and transportation was a problem for the colonists. For the corporation the urgent problem was providing subsistence and supplies to the various colonist camps. For the transportation of supplies the corporation hired two men, Earl McHenry and Bill Curtis. Both had light trucks and hauled supplies to the various camps on a daily schedule. When illness or other emergency required transportation of some individual or family, the corporation sent a pickup to the camp for transportation."

Life in the tent camps during the first few weeks was challenging, with firewood and water to haul, and deep mud from the cold and rainy weather, but the families made do, knowing their homes were being built and the tent camp situation was only temporary. The mosquitoes were relentless; almost twenty miles of mosquito netting was ordered, and the store could not keep up with the demand for citronella. The 16' by 20' tents were tight quarters for some of the larger families, but by stacking the cots on top of each other bunk-bed style the colonists made do with the space they had. University of Wisconsin professor emeritus Arnold Alanen described the situation in his article, *Midwesterners in the Matanuska Valley: Colonizing Rural Alaska during the 1930s*, written for *Perspectives in Vernacular Architecture*, Volume 8 in the series from the University of Tennessee Press titled *People, Power, Places* (2000):

"Journalist Schaleben described the tents as being 'pitched in exact alignment, so that their lines make a geometrical design no matter from which point you look.' Each tent was sixteen by twenty feet in plan; had five-foot high walls made of twelve-ounce canvas stretched over a wooden frame; was constructed on a poorly fitted, rough plank floor; and was divided into partitions by wood, canvas, or cloth. A Montgomery

Ward cookstove, a scuttle of coal, a washbasin, and two to six metal cots with mattresses were provided in each unit. The tents proved sufficient for families with five or fewer children, but were 'hardly adequate' for some people, such as the Bouwens from Rhinelander, Wisconsin, who had eleven offspring. Several families had to double up until additional tents were assembled. The tents could get 'almost unbearably hot' during the long daylight hours of the summer, but then could be freezing cold by autumn. Some colonists piled dirt around the base of the units to curtail the winds that swept through the canvas and threatened to blow down stovepipes. The soil, described as 'so fine[ly] textured any breeze gives it a ride,' often covered the tent floors with dirt."

Five plans for houses were offered to the colonists, each a single-family "rustic cottage" design developed by the FERA architects in Washington, D.C., working under David R. Williams. Most of the homes, which ranged in size from 900 to 1,500 square feet, were one-and-one-half story with rectangular or L-shaped floor plans, although a few were single-story homes. Constructed of log, frame, or a combination of both, the houses featured gable roofs; four of the designs were three-bedrooms with a combination kitchen and living room, storage room, and many built-in elements; the fifth was a similar four-bedroom design. None of the homes included indoor plumbing or bathrooms, but there were spaces for the future development of indoor bathrooms. Likewise, none of the original plans had a full basement, but some of the colonists elected to dig their own basements after the fact.

Construction of the houses was relatively swift because David Williams' plan for using prefabricated components was employed, and because he ordered an additional 225 WPA workers from California– plus almost 100 local workers and foremen– to expedite the building. Five portable sawmills whirred steadily, producing enough lumber and three-sided house logs to keep the construction crews busy building, and by the end of October the last colony home was ready for occupation. In addition, the workers had completed building the trading post, warehouse, and generating plant, and had begun work on the school, gymnasium, and creamery/cannery.

The barns built for the colonists' farms were of a standard design, 32' by 32' by 32' high, recommended to support a subsistence family farmstead as originally intended by the government planners. In *The Matanuska Colony Barns*, by Helen Hegener (Northern Light Media, 2012), Matanuska Valley historian James H. Fox explained the evolution of the design:

"It was the subsistence idea which was the basis for the design of the iconic Colony barn. Later complaints about the barns and the tracts being too small for a viable business farm can be traced back to this early yet quickly discarded idea.

"Practical or not, the barns were designed by architects living in the tent city under the direction of David Williams, who based the gambrel roofed, cubic design on advice from local Experiment Station founder and Alaskan agriculturalist M. D. Snodgrass."

The barns were constructed of three-sided spruce logs, cut and milled on each site, stacked ten feet high, with oakum placed between each course and steel pins inserted into holes drilled through the walls vertically. Foot-long spikes were driven into the logs for added stability. The floor of the barn's haymow sat on joists across the top level of logs, then a four-foot board-and-batten pony wall gave additional space for hay under the soaring gambrel roof.

Three other barn designs were also built, including four barns constructed with a unique barrel-vault roof which gave a greater storage area for hay, two stallion barns measuring 30' x 25' with a low-pitched gambrel roof, and an unknown number of smaller 16' x 20' frame construction barns. Other outbuildings included chicken coops, well houses, sheds, and of course, outhouses. Wells were driven to supply each farm with an adequate source of water.

The cost of the homes and farm buildings was reported in the 1950 study for the U. S. Department of the Interior by Kirk H. Stone, titled *Alaskan Group Settlement: The Matanuska Valley Colony*:

"Homes, barns, and wells cost more than was anticipated... The estimates in March, 1935 were $1100 for a home and well and $200 for a barn. These figures were revised in May to: $985 per house, 50 barns at $598 each, and material for 150 barns at $200 each, and $140 per well. Actually, the appraised costs in May, 1936 averaged: $1830 per dwelling, $506 for each barn, and $511 per well. The estimate on the barns was the only building cost anticipated accurately, but the barns were the buildings considered least suitable by the colonists."

As the families settled into life in the valley and the transient workers kept up a steady pace of building, Arville Schaleben's series of articles for *The Milwaukee Journal* related interesting news of the Alaskan colony for the many readers who were following the progress of the families:

"Several of the settlers have found their tracts too wet to work and have been relocated. Others have found their sections too rough for cultivation and have also been moved. The fact that the government owns most of the land in the valley makes such relocations a simple matter."

"Seventy cows and 69 horses arrived here Wednesday from Seward, having been brought there from Seattle on the North Star."

"The colony got its first industrial order Wednesday–for 25 carloads of mine props from Alaskan mining interests. The colonists will get 22 cents each for eight-foot spruce props. This will net each colonist about $30. These props will be ends left over from logs cut for homes and community buildings."

"The colonists have been taking advantage of the bright nights to hunt and fish, but a territorial game warden has broadcast that a license is necessary for hunting. A year's residence is necessary to obtain a license or a non-resident license can be purchased for $50. None of the settlers has $50 for such a purpose. The settlers had been potting spruce hens especially. Some have seen black bears near the camps and there are indications that there are moose around. There are no restrictions on fishing and the settlers have been dragging in the big ones throughout the valley."

The 1935 Matanuska Colony Project

"By the light of the soft midnight sun the Matanuska colonists Thursday remembered the brothers and fathers who died for them in the World War. They met in the tiny temporary recreation hall hammered together out of spruce logs and finished boards hauled into the valley by the railroad which runs one regular train a week. Under the sheltering canvas roof they bowed their heads and prayed and thanked God for the 'new chance' He had given them.

"Presiding was the Rev. E. J. Bingle, stumpy Presbyterian pastor who came with the first of the colonists and has tramped about in boots through the forest helping them with the many pioneering troubles that beset them."

On June 6th Schaleben detailed the first community council meeting in an article titled "Alaska Colony Organizes, Big Problem is Garbage:"

"Eighteen sturdy men and women made history Tuesday night out of garbage, dogs and cows. They comprise the first council of the Matanuska valley colony. Each camp selected one man and one woman delegate, except the headquarters camp, which, because of its larger population, got four delegates. This council will make rules of conduct for the new society and advise the Alaska Rural Rehabilitation Corporation, governmental sponsor of the colony, of knotty problems."

He continued the next day with a startlingly colorful headline: "Law in Alaska Colony is the Law of the Gun," followed by a report on an altercation which arose over loose dogs in the camps. A colonist suggested that if the loose dogs were not tied up by 9:30 or 10:00 at night, a .32 would solve the problem. "The way his cohorts cheered left no doubt about the acceptability of that type of enforcement."

On a lighter note, Schaleben filed this article which was published on June 8th, 'Dance Night in Matanuska New Thrill for Colony':

"It's dance night in Matanuska, the next village down the tracks, and the sign on our camp bulletin board says, 'Welcome Colonists! Bring Your Own Instrument If You Know How To Play.'

“So at 8:30, when here it's still light as afternoon in Wisconsin, we catch a ride to friendly Matanuska. Matanuska's dance hall is near the center of its 15 or 20 houses and half dozen frame business buildings. It is recently built, of lumber from razed buildings. Gray, black, and green painted boards squeeze in among many unpainted ones. Tarpaper shields the roof. The hall is decorated with American flags, and red, white, and blue bunting streamers stretch to a focal point in the center of the peaked ceiling.

“In one corner sits an upright piano, scratched and scarred. The only light in the hall, a gas lamp, rides atop it. The woman who handles the music box is gray haired and bursting with tunes. Standing around her and looking jazzy are two gents sawing on violins, and a fat accordion man.”

"Now they're doing ‘Goofus’ (remember it, back in 1930?) and keeping time with feet, arms, heads and hips. By and by they get waltzy and ease into ‘Down the River of Golden Dreams,’ and then do a little two-stepping with ‘When I was a Boy from the Mountains and You were Girl from the Hills.’ Later on somebody comes with drums. He knows ‘All the World will be Jealous of Me.’ He does it, and the crowd cries for more.

“Meanwhile, out on the floor, the boys are swinging their ladies, and their ladies are swinging them. ‘Round and ‘round, criss-cross, up and down, back and forth–flea-hoppers, one-steppers, two-steppers, a couple of charlestoners, and a gentleman in overalls who just walks forward and backward and varies that not a mite except for a little trotting in a stiff sort of way. There's a native Indian couple shuffling around. She's got on tennis shoes, he's wearing a buckskin shirt.

“‘Damn it, you don't dare cut in,’ says a colonist to another. But the fellow's had just enough Brigadier General (bottled, for you can't buy by the drink in Alaska), and he's game. He taps the buckskin shirt on the shoulder and bundles the tennis shoed one in his embracing arms.

“‘Let's dance!’ he shouts, and they do.

“Most of the women wear boots and breeches, but a few boast fancy dresses. They are flowered or striped or solid colored. Some of the colonists, and the resident women too, make mighty fine pictures a-whirling there on the floor. There are dudes among the men, in loudly striped suits and ties, but mostly there are just plain ordinary farm men in heavy boots and work clothes.

"Toward 2 o'clock the music stops. The sun starts coming out again, after only an hour or two of rest. Folks get int their cars and rumble home through wooded lanes; so ends dance night in Matanuska."

The colonists' camps were vibrant places where dozens of children and dogs raced and played as the women shared recipes along with the latest news from other camps. The men formed crews to cut logs for their homes and barns while developing croplands and pasture. They fished in the streams, and talked and played endless card games in the evenings.

A cartoonist for the *Cleveland Plain Dealer*, J. H. Donahey, wrote this description of the Palmer camp: "...rows and rows of tents, tractors, trucks and lumber, with a domestic touch of wash on the line, boys on stilts and babies in perambulators, overalled women running gasoline washing machines, boxes, crates, horses hauling timber, and more boys and girls on bicycles, velocipedes and stilts, carloads of freight, canned goods on the siding...

"Over at headquarters where Colonel Hunt of the Marines, Capt. Eugene Carr of New York and Don Irwin of the Alaska Agricultural Experiment Station were in charge, typewriters were clicking, architects were finishing plans for a hospital, schoolhouse, trading post, church, community hall, cannery, post office, cobbler's shop and a jail, all for the new community center surrounding the village green of Palmer."

Through shared hardships and hard work, community meetings, church services, and events such as dances in neighboring towns, the intrepid families who left their stateside homes and ventured north to Alaska were slowly building a new life in the beautiful Matanuska Valley, but there were rough seas ahead, and changes in the wind.

"It is surprising how well the valley has straightened itself out, considering the heterogeneous collection of marginal social cases shipped north in the party, and the crackpot ideas used for operating the colony." ~Herb Hilscher

Chapter Ten

Troubled Waters

All through that first summer Arville Schaleben's frequent front-page headlines in *The Milwaukee Journal* spoke volumes about events which were transpiring in the new community. On June 10, 1935, Schaleben wrote glowingly: "Wisconsin Colonists Find Soil of Alaska Ideal" and noted in the subtitle, "Best of Land Given Settlers." Another subhead in large type extolled "'Brother, Let Me Roll in It,' One Settler Exclaims on Seeing Rich Loam of Valley."

Schaleben's article explained: "You can't find a man among the unshaven, tobacco-spitting oldtimers who inhabit this wild Matanuska valley who speaks badly of its soil. Even the dour boys back in the hills, who since Klondike days have been 'clean mad for the muck called gold,' concede its fertility. Small wonder then that not one of the new colonists from Wisconsin, Michigan and Minnesota has uttered a complaint against the soil they have come to till."

At the end of the article the source of the headline quote was revealed to be a colonist whose farm would be located in the Bodenburg Butte area: "The colonists already have been amazed by the stories of how things grow–grass four and five feet high, beets as big as a man's head, strawberries the size of coffee cups. But when you see day merge into night and night merge into day with hardly an hour of darkness and when

Publicized pioneers. Although it has been four months since the arrival of the colonists, newsmen and photographers are still prevalent. ASL-P270-613 by Willis T. Geisman. ARRC Album, Mary Nan Gamble Collection, Alaska State Library.

you cup Matanuska's soil in your hands and sniff its sweetness, you're inclined to explode, as Perle Archer of Cumberland did, 'Brother, let me at that land. It's beautiful. It makes me want to get down and roll in it.'"

In the same June 10 article, Schaleben quoted a pre-colony pioneer who expressed hope–along with many other early settlers–of joining the co-operative marketing venture the colonists would be creating. Schaleben also gave indication of Don Irwin's hopes for the colony project, which were realistic given Irwin's position and experience at the Matanuska Agricultural Station: "Irwin plans that the colonists' main cash crops will be peas, cabbages, potatoes, carrots, parsnips, beets, turnips, onions, lettuce, and various berries and fruits. He expects wheat, oats, rye, hay, barley and flax to be principally for subsistence."

The Milwaukee Journal, June 12, 1935. By Arville Schaleben. "Alaska Project Lags Badly, May Be Caught By Winter. Shortage of Labor and Necessary Working Tools. Center and School Not Yet Started, Well Digging Slow, Homes May Not be Finished. Palmer, Alaska. (By Radio) A personal investigation of the entire Matanuska valley colonization project reveals that it is lagging in virtually all phases. It appears a certainty that the government can't make good on all its promises to the settlers this year and there is even danger that all may not get homes before snowfall, present facilities considered."

On June 19, Alaskan newspapers carried the story that two colonists, who claimed to represent forty other colonists, sent the following telegram to President Roosevelt, Alaskan Governor John W. Troy, Relief Administrator Harry Hopkins, and senators from their home states:

"Six weeks passed. Nothing done. No houses, wells, roads. Inadequate machinery, tools. Government food undelivered. Commissary prices exorbitant. Educational facilities for season doubtful. Apparently men sent to pick political plums. Irwin and Washington officials O.K. Hands tied: Request immediate investigation."

Colony Manager Don Irwin calmly pointed out that buildings were, in fact, being constructed, including a large school; and that the primary problem had been delays in shipping materials and supplies. This was reiterated by Colonel Westbrook, who added that the colonists were better provided for in Alaska than they had been at home. But they were still constituents of the U. S. Senators in their respective states, and when the pleas for an investigation reached their congressmen, a full reporting was demanded on the conditions in the colony.

As a result, Harry Hopkins sent a number of officials to investigate the situation, including a government trouble-shooter and a special inspection team, and subsequently multiple layers of authority were added to the colony management. By mid-July the project staff had burgeoned to include a general administrator and an assistant general administrator; division directors of construction, farming, procurement, architecture, and medical services; and an inspection engineer, a fire warden, and a transient's physician.

Compounding the confusion of that phalanx of officials was a situation aptly described by Don Irwin in *The Colorful Matanuska Valley*: "Rapid changes of policy by the Washington authorities caused confusion and discontent among the colonists. Seldom did a policy for the colony hold good for more than two to three weeks. This caused uncertainty in management and discontent in the minds of the colonists."

There was more, of course. Irwin outlined the troubles which beset the colony, including a lack of full authority delegated to the manager and no definite understanding between the FERA officials in Washington and the ARRC in Juneau as to which organization had the authority to direct the policies of colony management.

Schaleben shared his analysis: "There are three obvious reasons why the project–which in itself seems entirely practical–has hit rough going:

"First, inadequate or careless preparations for problems to be faced in a virtual wilderness–and an isolated one at that.

"Second, an unexpected wet spring which added tremendously to transportation problems in the valley.

"Third, mismanagement, probably not so much here on the scene as in shipping of supplies from the states."

Irwin had reported the confused shipments of supplies; harnesses for the horses arrived without collars, wagons were shipped without doubletrees and yokes, a diesel engine for the power plant and radiators for the school arrived before construction of either building was started. Despite repeated wires to the dockman in Seattle, no tools were shipped. Finally the incompetent man was fired and there was no more trouble.

On June 22 Schaleben reported that young Donald Henry Koenen, age 4, had died of "heart trouble, possibly aggravated by two weeks of measles." Three days later he would share details of the child's burial "...in a homemade wooden casket covered with wild roses and bluebells that his playmates had gathered."

At the end of the June 22nd article, which also announced that more workers were joining the project, Schaleben wrote, "Reports from Washington reaching here that there is a widespread epidemic of sickness among the colonists, or that many of them wish to be taken back home, have no foundation in fact, so far as can be learned. There seems to be no more than the normal amount of sickness, and most of the colonists like it here and wouldn't leave under any circumstances."

The Milwaukee Journal, June 29: "Alaska Colony Gets Promise of Real Action. New Coordinator Arrives and Tells Colonists That Houses Will Be Ready; Some Lose Credit."

The Milwaukee Journal, July 3: "Defers All Colony Work Except Homebuilding. Carr's Orders Delay Alaska School Project."

By the end of June several families were ready to return to the United States, citing illness and discontent as reasons for their discomfiture with the colony project. The families departed from Seward in early July, with their transportation as far as Seattle paid for by the colony management. The returnees were met by newspapermen eagerly seeking sensational stories, and the unhappy travelers, all too willing to pour out their woes, did not disappoint them.

The 1935 Matanuska Colony Project

On June 25 the *Ironwood Daily Globe*, in Ironwood, Michigan, ran an article about the situation in Alaska which was written for the Associated Press by Mrs. Lloyd Bell, one of the colonists from Minnesota. Titled "Most Colonists Pleased; Want Agitators Ousted," Mrs. Bell wrote amiably that the weather in the Matanuska Valley was wonderful, with hot days and cool nights, plenty of rain, and rapidly-growing vegetation. She explained that the mosquitoes were very bad in the timber, but added "they are no menace in the open and we are told with the settlement of the land they will be eliminated."

Expressing satisfaction with Alaska, she noted most of the colonists were 'well pleased' with the country, and added that her husband, Lloyd Bell, "says it would take a squad of soldiers to get him out of the valley." She continued, "Gilford Lemon, of Koochaching county, Minn., says he intends to stay 'until hell freezes over.' Many other colonists express similar opinions."

She went on to describe their daily lives: "Most of the colonists are still in their tents, but they are fixed very comfortably with board floors, doors, and screen windows. A library has been opened in the community hall, with a few books and lots of magazines.

"A bus line makes two complete tours of the different camp centers twice daily, and baseball games are played almost every Sunday. The children are having a glorious time, with large playground swings, teeter-totters, and games of kitten ball, horseshoes and marbles. Church and Sunday school are held every Sunday.

"There is much sickness but it is mostly measles, mumps, chicken pox and pink eye, and no serious diseases. Many should never have come here because of poor health. There are two doctors and one Red Cross nurse with the transient workers and they are aiding the colonists, too. There are at least five registered nurses among the colonists. A big complaint is that the doctor has no car of his own and the colonists are scattered all over the valley. Provisions are being made for about 15 teachers to come here for approximately 375 to 380 pupils in the fall. The school land is being cleared and more materials are arriving daily."

And then Mrs. Bell roundly addressed the malcontents:

"Several agitators in the colony are keeping things continually boiling. We would like to have them deported. There is cause for complaint here, but reports of conditions have been exaggerated.

"The construction work is slow, as wrong equipment and materials have been shipped. Mr. Irwin (Don Irwin, project manager) ordered wagons and received school furniture and gasoline tanks."

She summed up: "The colonists want United States control continued, with Mr. Irwin in complete charge. He is well liked by all the colonists."

There was no doubt that Don Irwin was liked and appreciated by the colonist families. He was an understanding and patient man, a hard worker, a fair administrator, and a very keen observer. A case in point was Irwin's descriptive appraisal of the *Milwaukee Journal* reporter, Arville Schaleben, in his book, *The Colorful Matanuska Valley*:

"He felt that this project rated something more than a few days of exciting, inflammatory headlines. He dug deeply into what was going on. He was not afraid to walk, thumb a ride on a Corporation truck, or borrow a horse from a Colonist to ride, if he could get the exact information he needed for his reports. It was not at all unusual to see Schaleben riding a horse bareback, at a lope, coattails, elbows, dispatch case and camera flying, hurrying to the railroad depot to file a deadline report for his paper. He was with the colony for four months. It is certain that the more conservative press in the South 48 states depended a great deal on information supplied by Schaleben through his *Milwaukee Journal* reports. It is also true that largely because of his honest and conservative reports a great many of the sensational headlines regarding the Colony lost their public appeal."

Throughout the summer of 1935, Arville Schaleben kept the Matanuska Colony in the headlines of the *Milwaukee Journal*, but he also devoted many columns of newsprint to sharing stories of the mundane, day-to-day lives of the Colony settlers. He wrote about the housewives tending their chores, the children playing games, a colonist being chased by a black bear, the workers building the homes, events in the community, the officials, the land, and even the weather. He punctuated his stories with photographs which added a visual dimension, with striking images of life in the Alaskan colony such as neat white tents in a row, transient workers heaving logs into place for a colonist's cabin, children playing marbles in the dirt, and scenes from the first funeral held by the colonists, for little Donald Henry Koenen.

Schaleben's headlines frequently ran on the front page of *The Milwaukee Journal*, telling the Colony story as it happened:

July 10: "Skeptic Lauds Colony Project. 'Nothing Wrong in Matanuska,' Former Michigan Governor Wires Roosevelt."

July 13: "Hammers Ring Out, Nurses Sprint; Presto! There's A Colony Hospital!"

July 14: "Politicians Go In Colony Shift. Things Humming as Fuller, Friend of President, Takes Control."

July 18: "Colony Gears Mesh Again. More Workers, Money Ordered by Fuller. Plan Big Hospital."

July 21: "Colony Houses Rushed in Big Push by Officials. Alaskan Winter Moving Closer, More Men to be Rushed to Valley to Shelter Families."

July 24: "11 More Families to Leave Alaska Colony on Saturday. Brings Total to 21 Quitting Relief Project."

July 27: "15 More Families Sail as Colonists 'Back Trail.' Alaskan Settlement Cut 15 Percent; Bear Enlivens Frontier, Pioneer Wife Faints."

July 28: "50 Dwellings Rise in Alaskan Colony as Bickering Disappears. Some Wells Are Finished. Settlers, Transients Losing Hatreds of Each Other in Race to Finish Before Snowfall. 'Big Shots' On Alaskan Frontier Get Colony Running Smoothly."

August 6: "Hail and Rain Slash Colony. Snow Blankets Mountains, Frost Nips Crops and Roads Are Bogs."

August 13: "Colony Future More Hopeful. Everyone Working Together at Last; the Officials Grow Optimistic."

The 1935 Matanuska Colony Project

On Thursday, August 13, 1935, a short item ran at the top of the front page of *The Milwaukee Journal*, bylined "By Special Cable to the Journal" and signed by Will Rogers, famous actor, author, humorist and social commentator, who had been contributing to the newspaper for nine years. Titled "Nothing to Do, So He Flies Over Peak," the article shared the travels of Rogers and his friend and pilot, Wiley Post, who were en route to Siberia for a holiday of hunting and fishing.

"Anchorage, Alaska. Well, we had a day off Wednesday and nothing to do, so we went flying with friends, Joe Crosson, who is Alaska's crack pilot and a friend of Wiley's and helped him on his difficulties up here on his record trips, and Joe Barrows, another fine pilot, in a Lockheed Electra. We scaled Mount McKinley, the highest one on the American continent. Bright sunny day, and the most beautiful sight I ever saw.

"Crosson has landed on a glacier over half way up in a plane and took off. Flew right by hundreds of mountain sheep, flew low over moose and bear. Down in the valley now. Out to visit Matanuska valley, where they sent those 1935 model pioneers."

At the bottom of the same front page, Arville Schaleben wrote about the visit, saying Col. Hunt and Eugene Carr had chauffeured Rogers, Post, and Crosson on a quick 90-minute tour of the colony, after which Rogers commented, "The valley looks great. It looks fine, fine. You got a mighty nice place here. We saw some colonists, caught one guy just moving his stove in. I said I'd just as soon be moving in with him."

An added short item at the bottom of Schaleben's report on Rogers' visit told of a community salmon canning and packing effort, led by the Rev. B. J. Bingle, with about 3,600 cans put up and "about 350 gallons salted, with more of that also done by individuals. The fishing was done on Knik Arm, an inlet from the ocean, and was a treat to most of the colonists, who had never done salt water fishing before."

The next morning *Milwaukee Journal* readers were startled to see a large quarter-page photo of Will Rogers and Wiley Post standing beside Post's airplane, under a bold black page-wide headline which read "Crash Kills Will Rogers, Post."

The beloved humorist and the flier who had circled the world had crashed on takeoff from beside a small river, where they had landed to inquire the way to their next destination, Point Barrow. It had been their intention to stop and visit the renowned trader and "King of the Arctic," Charlie Brower.

At the time of his death, the American people adored Rogers. He was the top-paid Hollywood movie star at the time, having made over 70 movies (including 50 silent films). He had traveled around the world three times, written more than 4,000 nationally syndicated newspaper columns, and had become a world-famous humorist and philosopher. He was a stout supporter of President Franklin D. Roosevelt and the leading political wit of the Progressive Era. He was mourned world-wide, and his presence, which had brought laughter and renewed hope at a time when the nation most needed it, would be greatly missed by the American public.

His lasting tribute to the Matanuska Colony was a one-liner in his final dispatch which mused, "There's a whole lot of difference in mining for gold and mining for spinach!"

Joseph Puhl, assisted by Henning Benson and Virgil Eckert, builds his home. ASL-P270-613 by Willis T. Geisman. ARRC Album, Mary Nan Gamble Collection, Alaska State Library.

"For many of us this venture is our last opportunity to provide security for our children and ourselves." ~Elmer J. LeDuc

Chapter Eleven

"Cabbages and Commissars"

An interesting sidelight, which escaped the attention of many, appeared below Arville Schaleben's article in the August 6 issue of *The Milwaukee Journal*. It was a short article datelined Anchorage, filed with the Associated Press, titled "Now They Talk of 'Super Colony.'"

The article explained that a colonization program on the Kenai Peninsula, along the lines of the Matanuska colony, was being considered by the government. Seward Mayor Don Brownell, who was returning from a trip to Washington, D.C., announced that federal officials were considering the transplanting of 2,000 families from various parts of the United States to the peninsula. Mayor Brownell said he thought the Kenai project preparations would more well planned than those at Matanuska had been. Apparently the discussions included acquiring all necessary land in advance, and building roads and constructing buildings before the colonists were brought to Alaska. Thorough examination of the applicants to show they had adequate "frontier farming experience," would be part of the new plan. No Kenai colony ever materialized, but the discussion of it was an interesting footnote to the Matanuska colony.

The article also noted that Don Irwin said 650 farmers, representing every state in the Union, had inquired about filling vacancies left by those departing the Matanuska Colony. "Some of the applicants 'almost pleaded for a chance,' said Irwin, and advanced their long experience 'on farming frontiers' as reasons why they should succeed in the government land settlement project." Irwin announced that the names of all the applicants for vacant farms at Matanuska would be filed, and they would form the basis for careful selection of colonists in any future plans. As it turned out, the selection process would begin only a few months later. In *The Frontier in Alaska and The Matanuska Colony*, Orlando W. Miller described the evolution of those who would come to be known as the replacement colonists:

"The... ARRC had to deal with the problem of replacing the colonists who had left the project. The departures continued irregularly until at the end of the first year of the colony sixty families had gone; nineteen more left in the second year and sixteen in the third. Had there been no replacements, the colony would have shrunk almost to disappearance and the houses and barns would have stood empty. However, despite jibes in the press, the first withdrawals at least helped the colony management by reducing the time and the amount of construction necessary before it could announce that all of the colonists were adequately housed and livestock sheltered."

For two years, from 1936 to 1938, the empty farms were taken over by families who were required to submit records of their farming and employment experience, their family histories, and a list of references. If they were not already in Alaska–and many were–they were required to pay their own way to the territory, and then they could take over an available farm tract under the same conditions of credit and aid offered to the original colonists.

As the ARRC terms for new farmers were altered over the next few years by adjustments in both expectations and agreements, the distinctive character of the original colony slowly faded. The corporation began to deal with the newer arrivals as simply farmers, and the original aspects of relief and rehabilitation were rarely mentioned. After a few years the term 'colonist' took on an entirely new meaning, and no longer indicated a wardlike dependency on the Corporation, but became instead simply a convenient way of identifying the early arrivals in the valley, just as the respected term 'pioneer' identified the venerable valley residents who pre-dated the colony project.

Throughout the late summer and early fall of 1935 the colonist families continued to work on their farmsteads, and from the vantage point of thirty-three years later, Don Irwin summed up the situation: "The summer was over. The efforts of the construction crews had produced excellent results. The families and livestock were under roof. There was a lot to be done by the individual families to finish the interior of their homes, but life seemed not so tense and the prospects looked much brighter even though their personal indebtedness was mounting."

The personal indebtedness of the colonists would be mitigated by a number of work credit and debt relief and reduction programs which would be put into place over the following years. Orlando Miller had a succinct explanation: "The management could bravely survive the first withdrawals of colonist families, describing them as the unfit, the troublemakers, but as the cost of the colony was increased by the efforts to hurry construction, it became obvious that the investment had to be protected. To allow the colony to collapse was politically unthinkable. With about 170 houses built and the community center developed, the colony had to be kept going in some way with a reasonable number of colonists, old or new. Thus, almost from the beginning, aid was granted beyond the original plans for the project..."

The original planners had estimated $1,093,365 for the colony, which included grants to the Alaska Rural Rehabilitation Corporation and to the Emergency Relief Administrations in the three states the colonists hailed from, Michigan, Minnesota, and Wisconsin. These funds were to cover administrative costs in both Washington, D. C., and Palmer, and the costs of developing the colony, which included the purchase of household goods for the colony families, buying the land, equipment, supplies, livestock, feed, transportation, the construction of farm homes and buildings such as barns, and the construction of the buildings which comprised the community center in Palmer. In addition, the projected amount was to cover operating capital for the new colony. But the planners undershot the mark several times over.

Kirk H. Stone's 1950 report, *Alaskan Group Settlement: The Matanuska Valley Colony*, prepared for the United States Department of the Interior, explained the situation:

"Financing the settlers was complex and costly. Most of the colonists interrogated feel strongly that this phase of colonization was the most important and the most poorly managed. When the colonists signed the Settlement Agreement they were told that their debt to the Cooperation would be about $3500 or less. Instead, many debts approximated $10,000 after two years of settlement and several were between $10,000 and $18,000. The result of high debts was discouragement for the colonists and at least half of those that left did so because they owed so much and felt that they would just get in more debt by staying in the colony. The blame for the high debt was partly the Corporation's and partly the colonists.' However, a fundamental cause was the hurried nature of the colonization and the significant point is the necessity of preventing a repetition of settlement in which haste, and therefore waste, is the rule."

Stone's report went on to describe some of the reasons for the high debt, including the expensive and reportedly inefficient non-colonist labor, the slow land clearing, the low quality of the livestock, poor economic management by some of the colonists, and interestingly, a series of efforts to control how the colonists handled their purchases.

In an effort to rein in the careless spending of some colonists, there were several attempts to provide substitutes for money. For example, at the trading post 'chits' would be signed for food, clothing, and other needed items; notes of credit were signed on the colonists' accounts for needed tools, building materials, and other supplies; and half of a colonist's payment for labor or for a sale would be credited to his account instead of paid directly to the colonist.

There was also a type of artificial money, brass and aluminum tokens called bingles, which were issued in several demoninations from March 1, 1936 to January 31, 1937.

In an effort to help the colonists control their rapidly mounting debts, each family was allotted a share of bingles equal to the amount of their budgetary allowance every month for purchases of goods at the trading post. The bingles–no relation to the Rev. B. J. Bingle–simplified the commissary accounting efforts, but the colonists despised the bogus money system and it was quickly abandoned.

Under the work credit program the colonists were advanced cash loans each month in proportion to the permanent improvements which were made on their farms, including land cleared, fences erected, or work done on buildings or equipment. This was an effort to provide some income for those colonists who were working full-time toward making their farms self-sustaining. Many were doing just that, but others, in spite of a policy ruling that no head of household could take a job away from his farm, were quietly seeking work off their farms in an effort to make ends meet and improve their lives. Jobs were available with the Alaska Railroad, the Alaska Road Commission, the coal and gold mines, and other entities.

In the later part of 1937, with the rising indebtedness of the colonists becoming untenable, all of the colonists' financial accounts were reduced by a Debt Settlement Program by which the Corporation assumed a portion of each colonist's debt. Included in the settlement were allowances for food and clothing since the beginning of the colony project, medical expenses incurred by the families, and charges for seed, feed, wells, building materials, and other items, the costs of which were not taken from the accounts registers, but were determined by a confusing method of appraisal. The total cost of the debt settlement was $1,137,560, and because all debts over $8,000 were reduced, there were valid complaints that the program favored those with greater amounts of debt, many of whom were considered irresponsible spendthrifts, while those who had shown restraint in their spending habits received less of a debt reduction.

The goal was to give each colonist family an indebtedness of around $5,000, an amount which officials felt the colonists could reasonably repay within the allotted 30 years of their Settlement Agreement.

There was a catch, however. The ARRC drew up a lengthy and sometimes rambling "Contract for Sale and Purchase of Realty" which those remaining in the colony were required to sign, and there were clauses in the contract which gave the colonists serious pause.

According to the terms laid out, once the colonist had paid the full purchase price for their farm they would receive a provisional warranty deed, but the property was to remain a unit of the "cooperative rural community." The farmer and his family were to become members of the Matanuska Valley Farmers Cooperating Association (MVFCA), use the land as their farm and home, follow good management practices under the direction and guidance of the ARRC, and not establish any business enterprise on their farm.

There were advantages and protections for the colonists also written into the contract, but there were details such as the colonist and his family would agree to live harmoniously with the other members of the community, the cooperative, and the corporation (although what that meant was not explained), and the corporation would have the right of entry to the property for inspection of the premises in order to carry out its supervisory duties. The contract also gave the ARRC the first option to buy the farm if it was offered for sale to a purchaser the corporation did not approve of, citing the "public trust and purpose" for which federal funds had been spent, and written into the contract was the power to evict a colonist for violation of the contract.

The realty contract was met with resentment, but with few options open to them, the colonists who remained all signed to become members of the MVFCA, which in later years became the Matanuska Maid Co-op.

When the press got wind of the new contract agreement there were agitated news articles quoting disgruntled colonists. One such unhappy settler, interviewed by Orlando Miller, called it "an attempt to mortgage the soul of the colonist and those of his family as well."

A few weeks after the renegotiated contract, and following an article in the magazine *Nation's Business* which accused the ARRC management of using the debt reduction program to force the colonists to accept the realty contract and membership in the new cooperative, Ted Leitzell, a writer for the high-profile literary magazine, *American Mercury*, traveled north to investigate the colony project.

Leitzell wrote a scathing article which was widely reprinted and circulated. He fiercely titled his article "Cabbages and Commissars" and sensationally compared the Matanuska Colony Project to Stalin's U.S.S.R. Appearing in the January, 1939 issue of the *American Mercury*, the article sparked widespread controversy with its fiery rhetoric:

"I find–to put it bluntly–that collectivism, following the Soviet pattern with the utmost fidelity, has come to the Matanuska Valley. Collectivism–and dismal failure. The experiment has been a flop financially, economically, and sociologically.

"With tactics warranted to bring a nod of approval from Stalin himself, the reluctant and unhappy colonists of Roosevelt's Alaskan adventure have been herded into agreements which leave them entirely at the mercy of the local New Deal commissars. They may not market their own produce; they must farm the way they are told; and, even after they pay for their land, they may be thrown off on 30-days notice if they displease the dictators in any way. They may not even sell their land, nor leave it to their children when they die, without the consent of the all-powerful who plan their daily lives for them. Dependent, for the very food they eat, the clothes they wear, upon the bureaucratic whims of the head collectivists, the colonists stumble through a dreary life on the government dole."

There were rebuttals to Leitzell's article, including one which labeled it a "masterpiece of distortion" and indignantly asked, "What right has the author blandly to label the colonists 'comrades?' What he leaves unsaid is equally calculated to mislead. Paragraphs might have been written about the richness of the soil, the business-like way of clearing the land, the blooded stock, luscious vegetables, community life, up-to-date school, and modern hospital. The spotlight is focused on mistakes made in the beginning, but nothing is said about how far the colony has already gone to rectify them."

An article by colonist wife Klaria Johnson, who had traveled to Alaska from Wisconsin with her husband, Victor, portrayed an exuberant joy in her newfound home:

"'Martyrs' with their lurid stories of danger, hardship, and injustice aroused more concern than the quiet, patient, pioneering-minded people who expected to put up with the bitter and the sweet. We colonists weren't really having a bad time. We went about building our home without the help of corporation carpenters–four neighbors went together. Each day I walked out to our tract and cooked lunch for the workers on a campfire under the birches. The fragrance of new-cut timber and moist earth, mingling with the good smells of coffee and frying bacon, will always be to me symbolic of those busy days of home-building and the high hope that was in us. Four months after landing in Palmer, we moved into our new house."

The newspaper and magazine articles seized on the colorful and dramatic news stories, while the colonists and the officials went about their business and shared their more mundane stories of hard work and increasing success. Slowly, learning as they went along, addressing issues as they arose, changing things as they could and working with what they couldn't change, those colonists who accepted the challenges were rewarded with accomplishment and progress. Forested wilderness gave way to fields and pastures, and lawns and gardens grew up around the colonists' homes. Roads were built and improved, livestock herds increased, and clubs and associations were formed to provide friendship, camaraderie, and support for each other.

Klaria Johnson wrote gaily about one such association, a homemaker's club, in an article for the *Anchorage Times*:

"Yesterday was club day. Work was hurried through in the morning and probably some of it was left undone. Lunch was set out for the family at home, and mother took a bowl of salad, a box of sandwiches, or a cake, and went to the club meeting. As many other women as could get away for the day were there. Housekeeping ideas were exchanged. Sewing demonstrations and short-cuts discussed. I learned how to put on a minute-and-a-half patch for overalls. How many hours since my marriage have I patched overalls and other work clothes? I never thought of such a quick, simple way to put on a patch. Noon came, lunch was served, cafeteria style. The coffee was hot and good. I noticed that the gowns were just as neat, haircuts just as trim, and faces as fresh as any ordinary group of women anywhere.

Is farm life in the Matanuska Valley lonesome and monotonous? No, indeed! Full and satisfying? Yes, most surely. Busy, healthy and cheery, with each day some task begun, each night to our beds, weary and contented."

The Matanuska Colony, launched in a heady atmosphere of publicity and public interest, became a 'must-see' stop for anyone visiting Alaska in an official capacity, and it was kept in the national glare to both its benefit and its detriment. The colony assuredly got off to a rocky start, for as Evangeline Atwood pointed out, "the very qualities for which the colonists were chosen to go to Alaska–independence, courage, self-sufficiency–proved to be stumbling blocks in the highly regimented and socially controlled regimes of some of the colony managers."

Added to that assessment was the honest appraisal of the first and most popular colony manager, Don Irwin: "In the early days of the Colony there was a high rate of resignations among General Managers of the Colony. Too often, decisions were made in Washington which could not be carried out practically in the field."

But in spite of the hardships, or perhaps because of them, the colonists persevered and built a community for themselves, their children, their grandchildren, and all who wished to join them.

"I wouldn't have missed the experience with the colony for a million dollars, but I wouldn't do it again for two million." ~Don Irwin

Chapter Twelve

Matanuska Colony Legacies

Each year, on the second weekend of June, the city of Palmer hosts Colony Days, a three-day celebration to honor and commemorate the town's Colony roots. A grand parade winds through the heart of town, the Colony House Museum holds an open house, a farmer's market and festival provides food and entertainment, and live music is everywhere. Games and contests, a fun run, a bike race, bed races, a salmon cook-off, sidewalk art for children, a quilt walkabout, and a custom car rally and show provide something for everyone. Palmer's Colony Days is a much-anticipated highlight of early summer.

The first Colony Day celebration–a single day event–was held on May 16, 1936, the first anniversary of the arrival of the colonists in the territory. Alaska Territorial Governor John W. Troy and Ernest Gruening, who was at the time director of the Division of Territories and Island Possessions of the Department of the Interior, but who would become Alaska's seventh governor in 1939, were the featured speakers.

The first Colony Day celebration marked the transformation of the colonists from residents of their home states of Michigan, Minnesota, and Wisconsin, to residents of the Territory of Alaska.

Buddy and Victor Yohn in their new cabin. ASL-P270-593 by Willis T. Geisman.
ARRC Album, Mary Nan Gamble Collection, Alaska State Library.

Another legacy of the times, the beginning of the Alaska State Fair, was described by Talis Colberg in an article for the *Mat-Su Valley Frontiersman*, published August 27, 2012:

"The history of the colony often eclipses the reality that there were many settlers in this Valley long before the colonists' arrival. Those pre-colonist settlers accomplished quite a lot. One of their most significant legacies is the Alaska State Fair. It is often incorrectly assumed that the colonists started the fair because that first fair opened in Palmer the year after the colony began. In fact, the fair was set into motion by the enthusiastic efforts of Milton D. Snodgrass and members of the Northland Pioneer Grange No. 1 in Palmer, an organization that still exists."

He explained that throughout 1936 Snodgrass lobbied hard for a fair, and finally this notice was recorded in the minutes of the Grange meeting for July 10, 1936: "Mr. Snodgrass reported that the committee was working on the fair. A meeting will be held at 7:30, July 11 in this hall to organize a Fair Association, all interested come. Plan Sept. 4 as opening day for the Fair. The committee is selling chances on a car to raise money. Drawing probably to be opening day."

The first fair was held on the grounds of the new Colony school, and Mr. Snodgrass hand-typed a 12-page exhibitor's guide and fair schedule, in which he was listed as director, president and manager of the fair. About 3,500 people came to the first fair, and most of the $6,000 raised went to pay exhibitor premiums and other costs.

Evangeline Atwood wrote about it in *We Shall Be Remembered*:

"The entire community participated in that first fair, making it a gala affair, with rodeo, races, movies, exhibits of agricultural products, handicrafts and foods. Virginia Berg was elected Miss Matanuska Valley and later won the title of Miss Alaska, in competition with queens from other Alaskan communities at the Fairbanks Ice Carnival. She was the territory's first 'Miss Alaska.'"

The first fair coincided with the opening of the Knik River bridge and the Anchorage-Palmer highway, the first road link to Anchorage. When the colonists arrived the only transportation link between the Valley and the rest of the territory was the Alaska Railroad and a handful of unimproved roads criss-crossing the valley. The railroad was the colony's first lifeline, bringing all of the building materials, supplies, food, equipment, workers, and the colonists themselves to Palmer.

After the colonists arrived, the Alaska Road Commission began the construction and improvement of roads in the valley. In 1935 and 1936, 47 miles of existing roads were improved by resurfacing them with gravel, and 31.8 miles of new roads were constructed. The new roads primarily provided access to the colonists' homesites, but some also connected the existing roads.

A road had been constructed from Anchorage to the Eklutna River in 1934, in part because an Alaska Railroad siding and station house had been built near the Eklutna village in 1918; and in part because the Eklutna Power Plant, which harnessed the power of the Eklutna River, was founded in 1923 by Frank I. Reed and developed into the Anchorage Light & Power Company. The 30-mile road provided access to both.

In 1935 funds were advanced to complete the last 20 miles of construction to the Matanuska Valley, which included bridging the Knik River at a point just below Pioneer Peak. The Alaska Road Commission opened the new Anchorage-Palmer highway at 10:00 a.m. on September 4, 1936. Colony Manager Ross Sheely and "Father of the Alaska Highway" Donald McDonald were among the speakers. An hour later the first Alaska State Fair opened its gates for a four-day run.

Don Irwin shared an interesting story about the Knik River bridge:

"In March 1936, the Knik River Bridge was under construction. Mrs. Lee Rees, who lived in Anchorage, was on her way to Palmer. She was driving five dogs hitched to a sled. She had tried to cross the river on the ice but found it too thin. She could see that the bridge was not complete but decided to see if she could cross. The bridge was decked about three fourths of the way from the south end. When she came to the end of the decking there was a sheer drop of about fifteen feet with only a ladder to climb up and down. The men working on the bridge asked if the dogs would bite. Mrs. Rees said the dogs were tired and thought they could be handled. Unhitching the dogs, the men carried them down the ladder one by one. The sled was let down; then Mrs. Rees climbed down. The dogs were again hitched and the lady was on her way to Palmer. The first team and vehicle had crossed the Knik River Bridge."

The Matanuska Colony was at the forefront of electrification of the valley. In 1935, President Roosevelt, a longtime advocate of cheaper electric power, signed an executive order creating the Rural Electrification Administration (REA), another New Deal experiment. The following year he signed a bill that allowed the REA to make low-interest loans available to electric cooperatives.

In 1937 the Matanuska Colony petitioned the REA for help in creating an electric cooperative, but their request was mislaid and not acted upon for three years. In 1940 colonist Walter Huntley received a telegram from the REA advising that the application was being considered, and on March 1, 1941, Palmer-area residents–largely comprised of colonists–formed the first REA cooperative in the Territory of Alaska, the Matanuska Electric Association (MEA).

Mr. Huntley, the first chairman of the MEA, sent the REA a telegram saying the Matanuska farmers were "READY PROCEED RURAL ELECTRIFICATION THIS VALLEY." Two months later, the Matanuska Electric Association borrowed an initial $140,000 from the United States of America, at 2.46 percent interest, to begin building electrical lines. On May 12, 1941, MEA signed its first power purchase agreement, arranging to buy electricity from the Anchorage Light and Power Company, generated by the Reed hydroelectric power plant at Eklutna. In 1942 the lines were activated with 150 customers on 93 miles of line; 31 were homes and 35 were farms. Within three years the number of customers had almost tripled.

When the Alaska Railroad laid rails through the Matanuska Valley in 1916, it brought lines for telegraph and telephone communications to each of the section houses and railroad stations along the route. Two years later, in 1918, the Agricultural Experiment Station at Matanuska was granted an extension line. When the Matanuska Colony's community center was built in 1936, a privately-owned family business was supplying commercial telephone service, which was installed throughout the colony buildings and connected to the lines operated by the Alaska Railroad and the Army Signal Corps.

Surplus Army field wire was then used to extend telephone communications to the outlying colony camps. Don Irwin explained in *The Colorful Matanuska Valley*, "It was hung on bushes, run through the timber or tacked on trees or posts to keep it working. Moose broke the wires, batteries went dead, and it was a poor substitute for a communication system. It served its purpose, however, even though crude, there were very few times when a long distance call or an emergency message did not reach its destination."

The Matanuska Telephone Association, a membership cooperative, was informally organized in 1954. There were other cooperatives in the valley, including the community hospital, several farm organizations, and a number of social and recreational associations.

The colonists' early struggles to build their farmsteads and make a living on the land saw a sea change in 1940 when the federal government, which considered Alaska a militarily strategic location, began construction of the Fort Richardson army base near Anchorage. The work, which included the construction of new airports and highways, was steady and reliable, and defense construction paid well.

Within three years 50,000 men were stationed at the army base, and thousands of civilians came to the area to provide support services. This created a ready market for everything the Matanuska farmers could produce, including milk, meat, eggs, vegetables, and other farm products. An acre of cabbage, celery or lettuce could bring a farm family thousands of dollars, and a new era of prosperity came to the colony.

Many farmers improved their facilities to Grade A dairy standards, and with the support of the very successful Matanuska Maid cooperative, dairy farming became the most dependable form of agriculture in the valley. According to one report, by 1966 there were 240 farms in the Matanuska valley, of which 42 were dairy farms, 22 raised potatoes, and 15 grew assorted vegetable crops. The remainder were not full-time farms.

Kirk H. Stone's 1950 report for the U.S. Department of the Interior, *Alaskan Group Settlement: The Matanuska Valley Colony*, summarized the findings of his eight years of interest in and work on Alaska, and three summers spent in the Matanuska Valley:

"The Matanuska Valley Colony has been an effective and generally successful experiment to increase permanent settlement in the Territory. In 1934 The Valley was a partly broken and isolated wilderness. At that time it was populated by about 500 people who did some farming in conjunction with mining, fishing, hunting, and trapping. In 13 years the eastern half of The Valley has become a widely broken and accessible forested area. In addition, The Valley has a population of 2500-3000 people who are participating in a growing farming economy and who work at various non-agricultural occupations. These changes have been made in an area of diversity that borders the northern limits of the inhabited Western world and they show that additional settlement is feasible there."

Five years later, in 1955, then-director of the Matanuska Experiment Station, Hugh A. Johnson, co-authored a study of the colony with Keith L. Stanton. Titled *Matanuska Valley Memoir,* the study detailed the history of the Colony project, assessed its impact on the valley, and then cautioned:

"Much ado is made that the Matanuska Valley, *as a result of the colonization program*, is the only prosperous agricultural area in Alaska. Sound reasoning fails to weigh adequately that the Colony was superimposed on a budding transportation system, on farms that had been established without subsidy and on an almost non-existent market. A more realistic analysis points out that the Colony and its $5.5 million investment *speeded up* development. The colonization program was saved by the unprecedented and unheralded establishment of nearby military bases and the attendant growth of local markets. The Colony may have been located by design; it was saved by luck."

Not content to simply point out the shortcomings of the Colony project, the authors then chastised the government planners:

"Government should be behind the entrepreneur helping him–not over him forcing him into a preconceived mold. It is very doubtful that any individual or any group is capable to plan finite details for a community. Broad definitions of physical conditions, integrated programs of public works related to speed of community needs and a policy of encouraging development through educational, financial or other necessary assistance should be the function of government. Details on individual farms belong to the individual family. This was not done in the Matanuska Valley Colony."

This pattern of either cautiously praising or roundly condemning the Colony Project would continue down through the years. Evangeline Atwood quoted Marquis Childs of the *St. Louis Post-Dispatch*: "Resettlement was a cozy conspiracy of good will to remake America on a cleaner, truer, more secure pattern."

Near the end of his treatise on the Matanuska Colony, *The Frontier in Alaska and the Matanuska Colony*, Orlando Miller observed: "Most of the colonists were probably not good enough farmers to proceed on their own; yet they were familiar enough with farming to resent guidance. They were largely rural residents and relief clients, but they came from an area with a fairly high level of living, and they expected cars, radios, telephones, decent roads, schools, and buses. They were accused by journalists and others of lacking pioneer qualities–that is, virtues. But they displayed other traits that may also have been characteristic of some pioneers–restlessness, impatience with careful routine, suspicion of authority, garrulity in discussing local civic affairs, a fondness for open country life, and a very moderate taste for farm drudgery."

One of the best and most accurate appraisals of the Matanuska Colony Project was written by a man who would win the 1944 Pulitzer Prize for Distinguished War Correspondence. In the late summer of 1937 this

American journalist, who wrote articles about the out-of-the-way places he traveled to and the people who lived there, visited the Matanuska Colony in Alaska.

A roving correspondent for the Scripps Howard newspaper chain, Ernest Taylor "Ernie" Pyle wrote in a folksy, friendly style, much like a personal letter to a friend. He'd been likened to the great storyteller Mark Twain for his sensible, down-to-earth missives. Ernie Pyle would go on to become a widely-known and well-loved war correspondent during World War II, reporting from both Europe and the Pacific, until his death in 1945 during a combat mission on a Pacific island.

In a two-part series published in late August, 1937, Ernie Pyle shared his perceptions of the Matanuska Colony:

"When I get back to the States, I know people will ask me, 'What is the truth about Matanuska?'

"Well, they won't get the truth from me. Because there isn't any one truth. It's like asking, 'What's the weather in Texas today?' There are a lot of answers, and all of them are right.

"Matanuska had had some merciless thrashing from its critics. And it has been overexaggerated in the other direction by its defenders. So I'll try to sift out the wheat from the goats, as the saying goes, and tell simply how Matanuska strikes me, a pure outsider who doesn't care one way or the other. Here are a few impressions:

"1–Matanuska Valley is certainly Alaska's 'Garden of Eden.' It is really a thrilling beautiful spot.

"2–Climatically, Matanuska is a better spot to liver than northern Minnesota.

"3–Good farmers can undoubtedly make a fair, but limited, living here.

"4–Bad farmers can't do any better here than anywhere else.

"5–Every man and woman in the valley I've talked with, even the ones who say they aren't doing any good, say they absolutely love Alaska.

"6–You hear reports that the government will abandon Matanuska, but I don't believe it.

"7–The success or failure of the project should not be judged, it seems to me, by the number of people who went back home. (A lot of them 'just came for the ride.')

"8–The government is now on its fifth million up here, and a great deal of it has been waste.

"The spending cannot be justified merely on the basis of re-establishing 200 families who were on relief.

"That last item raises the whole question of why Matanuska was established.

"To begin with, the government men admit that these 200 families could have been resettled somewhere in the States much cheaper, and possibly better.

"But the government wants Alaska colonized, and I suspect that the chief reason is military. Alaska is a big country with only 30,000 white people. It produces practically nothing for itself."

Pyle then explained how Alaska was like a far-away hand on a slender arm, dependent on the thin artery of steamship lines from the west coast. He noted that it would be 'easy to chop that hand off.' He explained that only by adding more people and becoming self-sufficient could the 'hand' become stronger.

"The government looks upon its five millions as applied not just to Matanuska, but as a prime that will sprout voluntary Matanuskas in many Alaskan valleys.

"That's why I can't get excited over the expense at Matanuska. Suppose it has cost five million dollars? Five million is unquestionably too much for homes for 200 distressed farmers. But also, 35 millions is too much to spend on a battleship just to make a home for 1000 sailors, if you look at it that way."

Ernie Pyle went on to describe the valley, the climate, and the colonists themselves. "Houses are thicker than in any farm community I've ever seen. Nearly every colonist has a very close neighbor. Each farm is only 40 acres, and colonists built in corners of their tracts next to each other."

Pyle noted that almost every farm had "from one to three good old-fashioned shepherd or collie dogs," and added an aside that there was rumored to be "a great deal of running around with other men's wives at Matanuska."

He compared the number of colonists who originally came north to those remaining, and enumerated the reasons why many left, noting "there were a couple of dozen reasons why people left, many of them perfectly legitimate."

According to Pyle, "A good many came down with that devastating disease known as homesickness, and simply couldn't stay so far away."

For those who chose to stay, the Matanuska Valley, with its towering mountains and shining lakes, gravelly braided rivers and seemingly endless forests, became home. They stayed for as many different reasons as the other families left, each finding ways to make their hopes and dreams turn into reality for themselves and their children, and their children's children.

Today the Matanuska Valley is a vibrant, bustling place, and the city of Palmer, still framed in breathtaking beauty, boasts a population of over 6,000 people. The Colony farms with their large iconic barns are still readily evident, and agriculture still plays an important role in the local economy. The annual Colony Days celebration is bookmarked by the Colony Days Christmas event, another delightfully joy-filled occasion.

The Alaska State Fair has grown to become the largest single event in the state, and since 2000 the Fair has presented an annual Farm Family of the Year award to honor an Alaskan farming family which epitomizes the spirit of the industry, and to show appreciation for the thousands of hardworking Alaskans committed to agriculture.

The Alaska Rural Rehabilitation Corporation (ARRC) is still active and assisting farmers statewide, making loans to the agricultural industry in addition to housing, commercial fishing, and timber loan programs.

The Matanuska Experiment Farm, now a part of the University of Alaska Fairbanks' Agriculture and Forestry Experiment Station, provides research in sustainable agriculture, land reclamation and other environmental issues. The Matanuska Experiment Farm also supports and provides public access to the Matanuska Greenbelt, a unique 33-mile trail system maintained in partnership with several other institutions, which meanders across the Farm's fields and pasture lands, through boreal forests, past several scenic lakes, and over the rolling moraines left by the glaciers of the last Ice Age.

Don Irwin wisely wrote in *The Colorful Matanuska Valley*, "In ten years the public had forgotten that John Jones or Jim Baker had been Colonists; they were Alaskans."

Just so. Alaska has always been a great melting-pot of those who've come north for a myriad of reasons, and while the Matanuska Colony garnered a lion's share of publicity in its heyday, the Colonists themselves settled comfortably into the Valley and have become just another part of Alaska's colorful history. Today there are roads, parks, schools, businesses, and many local landmarks named for the Colony families, tangible reminders of the Matanuska Valley's extraordinary past.

The Matanuska Colony Project was an unusual social experiment by the American government, and it became a unique chapter in Alaska's history. Created in a bold vision, launched in a bureaucratic morass, steeped in controversy, and all the while nurtured by hopes and dreams, this unprecedented and unparalleled program changed the lives of hundreds of families, and thousands of people.

The Matanuska Valley–indeed, all of Alaska–has greatly benefitted.

Bibliography

Alanen, Arnold R. *Midwesterners in the Matanuska Valley: Colonizing Rural Alaska During the 1930s* (Article. *People, Power, Places.* University of Tennessee Press, Knoxville, TN 2000)

Atwood, Evangeline. *We Shall Be Remembered* (Alaska Methodist University Press, AK 1966)

Cole, Fox, Lane, Lee, Willingham. *Evaluation of Historic Sites in Palmer, Alaska* (Matanuska-Susitna Borough Division of Cultural Resources, Palmer, AK 1988)

Fox, James. *The First Summer: Photographs of the Matanuska Colony of 1935* (Alaska Rural Rehabilitation Corporation, Palmer, AK 1980)

Geisman, Willis T. Mary Nan Gamble photograph collection. 976 b&w photographs documenting the Matanuska Colony Project. (Alaska State Archives, Alaska State Historical Library)

Hegener, Helen. *The Beautiful Matanuska Valley* (Northern Light Media, AK 2014)

Hegener, Helen. *The Matanuska Colony Barns* (Northern Light Media, AK 2013)

Hoagland, Alison K. *Buildings of Alaska* (Oxford Univ. Press, NY, 1993)

Hulley, Clarence C. A *Historical Survey of the Matanuska Valley Settlement in Alaska* (from The Pacific Northwest Quarterly, Vol. 40, No. 4. Oct., 1949)

The 1935 Matanuska Colony Project

Irwin, Don. *The Colorful Matanuska Valley* (Don Irwin, AK 1968)

Johnson, Hugh A., and Jorgenson, Harold T. *The Land Resources of Alaska* (University Publishers for the University of Alaska, NY 1963)

Johnson, Hugh A., and Stanton, Keith L. *Matanuska Valley Memoir: The Story of How One Alaskan Community Developed* (University of Alaska Experiment Station, Palmer, AK 1955)

Kari, James, and Fall, James A. *Shem Pete's Alaska: The Territory of the Upper Cook Inlet Dena'ina* (University of Alaska Press, AK 2003)

Kirker, Lorraine M. and Lynette A. Lehn. *Matanuska Colony 75th Anniversary Scrapbook* (Alaskana Books, Palmer, AK 2010)

Lively, Brigette. *The Matanuska Colony: Fifty Years 1935-1985* (Matanuska Impressions Printing, AK 1985)

Matanuska-Susitna Borough. *Knik, Matanuska, Susitna: A Visual History of the Valleys* (L&B Color Printing, Wasilla, AK 1985)

Miller, Orlando W. *The Frontier in Alaska and the Matanuska Colony* (Yale University Press, New Haven, CT 1975)

Potter, Louise. *A Study of a Frontier Town in Alaska: Wasilla to 1959* (Roger Burt Printing, Hanover, NH 1963)

Potter, Louise. *Old Times on Upper Cook's Inlet* (Book Cache, AK 1967)

Stone, Kirk Haskin. *Alaskan Group Settlement: the Matanuska Valley Colony* (U.S. Dept. of the Interior, Bureau of Land Management, Washington, DC 1950)

THE 1935 MATANUSKA COLONY PROJECT

The Remarkable History of a New Deal Experiment in Alaska

by Helen Hegener

Additional copies of this book
are available for $24.00 postpaid from:

Northern Light Media
PO Box 298023
Wasilla, Alaska 99629

http://northernlightmedia.wordpress.com
email: northernlightmedia@gmail.com

Other titles available from Northern Light Media

- *The Matanuska Colony Barns: The Enduring Legacy of the 1935 Matanuska Colony Project*
- *The Beautiful Matanuska Valley*
- *Along Alaskan Trails: Adventures in Sled Dog History*
- *The All Alaska Sweepstakes: History of the Great Race*
- *Long Hard Trails and Sled Dog Tales*
- *Appetite & Attitude: A Conversation with Lance Mackey* (DVD)

The 1935 Matanuska Colony Project

21862491R00085

Made in the USA
San Bernardino, CA
09 June 2015